THE RECESSION-PROOF BUSINESS

THE
RECESSION-PROOF
BUSINESS

Lessons from the Greatest
Recession Success Stories
of All Time

VICTOR CHENG

Innovation Press

San Francisco

This book and the information contained herein are for informative purposes only. The information in this book is distributed on an "As Is" basis, without warranty. The author makes no legal claims, express or implied, and the material is not meant to substitute legal or financial counsel.

The author, publisher, and/or copyright holder assume no responsibility for the loss or damage caused, or allegedly caused, directly or indirectly by the use of information contained in this book. The author and publisher specifically disclaim any liability incurred from the use or application of the contents of this book.

All rights reserved. No part of this book may be reproduced or transmitted in any form by any means, electronic, mechanical, photocopying, recording, or otherwise, without the prior written permission of the publisher.

Throughout this book trademarked names are referenced. Rather than putting a trademark symbol in every occurrence of a trademarked name, we state that we are using the names in an editorial fashion only and to the benefit of the trademark owner with no intention of infringement of the trademark.

Published by Innovation Press, 182 Howard Street, Suite #185, San Francisco, CA 94105

Printed in the United States of America

ISBN 978-0-9764624-2-2

For Julia, Alex, and Charlie

About The Author

Victor Cheng, former McKinsey consultant, is renowned for helping business owners turn around and grow their businesses during the toughest economic times. He has been featured as an expert on marketing in a recession by the Fox Business Network, MSNBC, *The Wall Street Journal*, *SmartMoney* magazine, and *Inc.* magazine.

Victor has also been a featured speaker at the Harvard Business School and is a graduate of Stanford University.

Bonus Items

Additional recession survival strategies, tips, and examples that could not be included in the book are available from the author's free email newsletter. Subscribe by visiting www.askvictor.com.

CONTENTS

PREFACE...I

PART I: THE RECESSION-PROOF FORMULA........1

1) RULE #1: ADOPT THE RECESSION-PROOF MIND-SET..2
2) RULE #2: SOLVE A PROBLEM THAT GETS WORSE
   IN A RECESSION..20
3) RULE #3: MAKE YOUR BUSINESS
   COMPETITION-PROOF....................................28
4) RULE #4: MARKET MORE AGGRESSIVELY,
   NOT LESS...40
5) MORE RECESSION SUCCESS STORIES........................50

PART II: RECESSION MARKETING...................64

6) HOW TO CHANNEL CUSTOMER DEMAND.................66
7) HOW TO WIN OVER CUSTOMERS...........................72
8) MAKE MARKETING AN INVESTMENT,
   NOT AN EXPENSE..90
9) MARKETING IS ALL ABOUT TIMING.......................100
10) THE CHIEF RAINMAKING OFFICER.......................106
11) UNLOCK THE HIDDEN PROFITS
    IN YOUR BUSINESS.......................................114

PART III: BUSINESS REINVENTION..................142

12) BUSINESS REINVENTION....................................144
13) RESOURCES FOR BUSINESS REINVENTION..............160

Preface

"Victor, they're scared out of their minds." Normally when I go on stage to give a speech to a group of business owners and CEOs, I'm the one who is a bit nervous. But the person introducing me that evening was pointing out that the audience was a lot more nervous than I was. They were all deeply worried about what was, for most of the audience, the worst economic crisis of their lifetimes.

I went up to give my speech and afterward, I was surprised and touched by the response. Dozens of people came up and thanked me for giving them hope about getting through this recession. I had not intended to give a "motivational" speech – one high on energy and low on facts or actionable advice. Rather, my goal was to share the results of my research on small and medium-sized companies that did extremely well in the recessions of the past – and to spell out in simple English the four things all these companies did in common to prosper.

The best way to describe the reaction of the audience after my speech was the word "relief." As explained to me, they suddenly had an accurate view of their situation, knew what to do to fix it, and could channel all that nervous energy into taking proven actions to protect their businesses. For them, this was invigorating and motivating, especially after being shell-shocked by a barrage of negative news headlines for weeks.

To fully understand why this book is likely to be useful to you, it's helpful to understand the entire story of how the research project that forms the foundation of this book came to be – and my deeply personal reasons for sharing it with you.

I assure you that when all the pieces come together, you'll see why the story is relevant to your life and business.

It all began on September 10, 2008. In every major crisis, there's a defining moment. And for me that moment was at 8:30 a.m. EST, when Wall Street giant Lehman Brothers announced it was in serious financial trouble. The announcement was significant for two reasons.

Lehman Brothers would become the first major financial institution that the US government would choose *not* to bail out in this recession. Investors suddenly realized that Lehman Brothers owed money to all the other major financial institutions around the world – institutions that would no longer be paid. In turn, these other firms would be unable to meet their financial obligations to account holders, clients, and yet more firms.

A legitimate and massive panic was set in motion – and fear prevailed that all the major financial institutions around the world would fail in one massive global domino effect. The results were financially devastating. Stock markets around the world simultaneously dropped by half, and trillions in US and global wealth instantly evaporated in the span of 30 days.

This moment was also significant for more personal reasons. At precisely 8:30 a.m. EST, I was in a studio for the Fox Business Network, about to appear live on a nationally televised broadcast, to provide my expert commentary on what banks should do to market themselves in a recession. I actually heard the Lehman Brothers news via my earpiece.

In the chaos that ensued, I suddenly realized that this recession would be much more severe and last longer than I had originally anticipated. I also realized that the rules of what it takes to run a successful business had been instantly rewritten. While certain business fundamentals would continue to be timeless, it was obvious that for many companies, "business as usual" was simply not going to cut it.

As an executive coach working exclusively with CEOs and owners of small and medium-sized companies, I knew that all my clients would be asking me what this financial meltdown meant and what they should do about it. In my coaching practice, the recession would quickly become the most asked about issue, trumping all others. At that time the crisis was so extreme that it was the worst one I'd seen in my lifetime. Even worse was that my own mentors, who are all considerably older than I am, felt that it was the worst economic event they had seen in their lifetimes. Not a pleasant thought, I assure you.

When the road ahead is unclear, I've found it's often helpful to take a look back at history for answers. I immediately started an internal research project to analyze the last 12 recessions going back 136 years in US economic history. I specifically wanted to find examples of companies that had begun as small businesses during a recession, depression, or economic panic and had generated hundreds of millions, and in some recent cases, billions, in sales in a down economy.

Happily, I found dozens of famous companies that started and prospered under economic conditions that the average person would consider incredibly hostile to business. Against all odds, these companies succeeded.

All the companies I discovered shared the same four commonalities. Unintentionally and without exception, all these recession success stories followed the exact same winning "formula" to recession-proof their businesses.

The companies featured are all billion-dollar businesses. Most are stand-alone companies on the Fortune 500 list. Others are now divisions within Fortune 500 companies.

Since this book is targeted at CEOs and owners of small and medium-sized businesses, you may be wondering what these big company success stories can teach you about what to do with your business right now.

The point I want to emphasize is that all the "big companies" were once small – possibly even smaller than your business is right now. When we hear names like Disney and Federal Express, we tend to think of industry giants. In this book, you'll see them as they once were – small businesses facing incredibly challenging economic conditions. The circumstances these winning companies faced at their inception were not too dissimilar from what you face today – massive economic upheaval of every variety, major reduction in customer spending, and tightly constrained resources. Sound familiar?

Philosopher George Santayana once said, "Those who do not learn from history are doomed to repeat it." I like the corollary to that statement: Those who remember, and learn from, history's success stories, are destined to repeat it.

I don't claim to be an economic historian. Instead, I see myself as a practical businessperson, an executive coach to others, and one that due to incredible economic circumstances, has become a reluctant historian. Extreme times call for extreme measures – and often these measures/insights come from history. So I've put on my historian hat, for no other reason than it was necessary, and I got tired of waiting around for someone else to do it for me.

Finally, through an incredible quirk of fate, or economic mismanagement (depending on your point of view), I find myself unusually, possibly uniquely, qualified to interpret these Fortune 500 lessons for you. I don't say this because of an overblown ego, but rather out of surprise that no one else has figured out these lessons and gone on to publish and publicize them first. Many authors write the book they wish someone else had written first – so they wouldn't have to! I am no exception.

The only reason I did the research behind this book is because I wanted to use those answers and share those insights with my clients.

But to understand why I've taken the considerable effort to write and publish this book rather than keep these insights as proprietary secrets, you'd have to understand my background.

On October 19, 1987, the stock market "crashed" by what was then considered a dramatic 22 percent. I saw firsthand the impact the crash had on my parents, who were small business owners. They lost a quarter of their life's savings in 24 hours. Days later, their top salesperson, who generated 35 percent of revenue, quit – taking with him nearly all the profit from my parents' business.

The stress was particularly hard on my father, who started to complain of chest pain. He went to see a cardiologist and had to wear an EKG device to record his heart rhythm over an extended period of time. The image of him wearing this hardcover book-sized device, with wires running all over his chest, is one that stays with me decades later.

We were lucky – it turned out his heart was physically fine. His pains arose out of the acute stress he felt at having his life's work seemingly go up in a puff of smoke in 24 hours.

A year later, the markets recovered fully. My parents were able to hire a new salesperson, someone who was even better than the one they lost, and life went on fairly well. But I never forgot the stress and strain the whole ordeal had placed on my parents and the spillover effect it had on my brother and me. My father's *reaction* to the economic conditions of 1987 had a much larger impact on our lives than the economy did.

This very distant memory, and the hope that I could prevent another family from experiencing such anxiety, wound up being part of the inspiration for writing this book, rather than making the insights available only to my clients.

Years after "Black Monday," as October 19, 1987, would be named, as an economics major at Stanford, I was fortunate to take a macroeconomics course from Donald Kohn, who was on a sabbatical from the Federal Reserve. At the time, he was Alan Greenspan's top in-house economist. And in addition to sharing basic macroeconomics theories from textbooks, he would provide firsthand accounts of the workings of the Fed and insider thoughts on Greenspan's interactions with Congress. Today, Donald Kohn is the vice chairman of the Federal Reserve – the #2 guy behind Bernard Bernanke, the current chairman.

I found those insights to be revealing all those years ago and consistent with what I see today. Given the choice between *actually* solving an economic problem and *appearing* to solve the problem (perhaps in a way that doesn't actually do anything), many politicians will choose the approach that plays better with voters – regardless of actual economic merits.

Unfortunately, this creates an awful lot of misinformation that ultimately finds its way to business owners like you. Programs that seem like they would help boost the economy may not do so, and programs that seem mundane may actually be very effective. Having the background to sift though all this provides a useful perspective I'll be sharing with you in the chapters that follow.

But, first, let me get back to my story and how it's relevant to you. In my first job out of college, I joined

McKinsey & Company, the famous management consulting firm whose alumni have held more than 70 Fortune 500 CEO positions.

On one of my first projects, I happened to be assigned to a major bank that was considering getting into subprime lending. The year was 1996 and it was my role to figure out how the subprime business worked and whether it was worth entering that market. I got an up close and personal understanding of the subprime industry in its infancy and the related practice of selling loans to Wall Street – another trend that was beginning to emerge at that time. Through that work, I developed a deep appreciation for the severity of the risk involved in combining those activities.

Over a decade later, this experience has given me a unique perspective on how our current economic crisis was triggered and how it has rippled through the global economy. For what it's worth, the popular perception that the Wall Street bankers were merely greedy is incorrect. They were greedy and incredibly stupid – not a good combination. More importantly, this background allows me to see with greater clarity how this whole mess does, and does not, impact business owners like you.

As if that weren't enough, the media has been making an already bad recession worse.

As my expertise about marketing in a recession became known to the media, many sought me out as an on-air expert and source. For example, I've been featured as a guest expert on marketing by the Fox Business Network, *The Wall Street Journal*, *Inc.* magazine, and *SmartMoney* magazine.

Through these experiences, I've gained insight into how producers and editors decide what's important enough to become the news. While I could write an entire book on that topic, I'll give you the most important insights. Bad news gets broadcast with a megaphone, while good news gets whispered. This happens because bad news drives up ratings and viewership more than good news does. Unfortunately, this negative bias creates a huge emotional roller-coaster ride experience for viewers like you.

In the many speeches I've given to business owners and CEOs on this topic, I've found that the level of anxiety experienced by audience members is much greater than the facts would warrant. It was only through the Q&A portions of the speeches that I came to understand that business owners feel like they're driving on a bumpy road blindfolded. Sure, the road conditions aren't great, but not being able to see the road due to the blindfold makes it 10 times worse.

While I can't change the condition of the road for you, I can certainly help you get rid of the blindfold that's getting in the way of your understanding of what's going on and share with you the lessons of how some famous companies have navigated through economic conditions similar to what you're experiencing now.

While my professional experience started in the upper echelons of the Fortune 500, my passion has always been in working with smaller companies. After McKinsey, I was on the executive team of two publicly-traded NASDAQ companies – running a $20 million a year division of one and serving briefly as chief technology officer and head of product development for another. This was in addition to starting three companies of my own.

Today, I'm an executive coach who guides CEOs of small and medium-sized companies in making the difficult decisions necessary to take their company to the next level. That next level ranges from economic survival to generating aggressive growth despite the recession.

While I certainly had the credentials, talent, and skills to work with the biggest companies in the world, I didn't find it satisfying. Somehow, helping a $10 billion company make an extra $10 billion in sales was not nearly as gratifying as helping a small business owner increase sales from $100K to $200K or the owner of a mid-sized firm grow in sales from $5 million to $10 million annually.

While the math of doubling a business is the same, the personal satisfaction is entirely different. With the big companies, the accomplishment has very little visible human impact. For the owners of smaller companies, doubling one's income is life-changing. Seeing someone's life improve significantly because of some contribution you made is profoundly rewarding. I hope to be worthy enough to consider it my calling.

As you can see, I'm passionate about business and the potential it has to have life-changing impact on one's life and that of one's family. As I child I was certainly on the receiving end of both the good and bad experiences – and much prefer the good experiences.

Today, I coach owners of small and medium-sized businesses on making the "do or die" decisions that can make or break a company. Unfortunately, with the current economic conditions, many businesses are facing these major decisions without being equipped with accurate facts and a clear, levelheaded, and unemotional perspective.

This too is the motivation behind sharing my message – a message that some describe as a message of hope grounded in economic and historical facts. Hope without facts is just a dream. Hope with the facts on your side is a plan. It is my goal that this book will provide you with the foundation for a plan to help you survive, and even prosper, in the worst of recessions.

I've organized this book into three sections. The first section explains what I call the recession-proofing formula. This "formula" is based on the greatest recession success stories of all time. It identifies the common thread amongst companies such as Disney, UPS, Charles Schwab, Hewlett-Packard, *Fortune* magazine, FedEx, Vanguard Funds, Pringles, and numerous others. They either started or had their formative growth years during one of the major recessions in the past 136 years of US economic history. This section provides the "big picture" overview of what separates the "winners" from the "losers" in a recession. It provides you with a set of useful and practical rules to guide your decision making.

The second section specifically covers the topic of sales and marketing in a recession. While sales and marketing is vital in a booming economy, it's doubly so in a recession for the simple reason that a major reconfiguration of market demand occurs in a recession. And it's your sales and marketing efforts that will first come in contact with this change and will be the first part of your business that needs to adapt to new market conditions. For this reason, it's the "tip of the spear" to fight your way through any economy undergoing significant change.

The third section focuses on business re-invention. For businesses that are struggling in a recession, the key next step is to reinvent your business to be in alignment with how customers are spending money right now – not when the economy was going through a boom, but right now. This section shows you the process and resources you need to follow to reinvent your business.

Finally, to receive free email updates to this book and alerts on newly discovered recession survival strategies, sign up by visiting www.askvictor.com.

Let's get started and discuss the key lessons learned from the greatest recession success stories of all time.

Part I:
The Recession-Proof Formula

CHAPTER 1

Rule #1:
Adopt the Recession-Proof Mind-Set

The first rule of the recession-proof formula is to adopt what I call the recession-proof mind-set. For someone that's very left-brain oriented (the logical part of your brain), I normally do not talk about "woo woo" soft stuff like mind-set and attitude. I certainly never did that when I first started coaching clients. But, over time, I've changed my perspective on this, after seeing many a talented business owner fail to succeed given a lousy, self-defeating attitude.

Similarly, I've seen successful entrepreneurs with surprisingly modest talent but with incredible levels of passion, tenacity, and aggressiveness that defy all logic. From a financial statement analysis perspective, the right mind-set and attitude makes a surprising amount of difference. Here's why.

Creating a recession-proof business comes from two places: 1) how you think and 2) how you act. At first these seem like two different activities, but they are actually intertwined.

As you'll discover, surviving and prospering in a recession requires you to force your company to adapt, and adapt quickly, to new market conditions – avoiding major threats while going after silver lining–type opportunities. So, without question, the ability to act quickly is essential to survival. However, if you, as a business owner and CEO, have the wrong mind-set, you will be slow to spot both the threats and the opportunities – and even slower to act upon them. Speed, both in decision making and in taking action, is a markedly essential asset in a recession, and the right mind-set helps enormously in this regard.

In short, the right mind-set leads to the right action at the right time. Here are four tips for adopting the right recession-proof mind-set:

1. There's still money out there, but you have to go find it.

2. Base business decisions on facts, not headlines.

3. Exploit the opportunities that recessions create.

4. Adapt or die.

Mind-Set Tip #1:
There's Still Money Out There,
But You Have to Go Find It

In the typical US recession, the economy shrinks 1-2 percent from start to finish. In a very severe recession, the economy will shrink 5 percent. Based on the information available at the time of publication, it's clear that the "great" recession of 2008-2009+ will fall into the severe category.

For a $14 trillion economy, that means the economy will shrink by $700 billion dollars. When most people, especially people in the media, see these numbers they immediately focus on the $700 billion in economic activity and spending that's disappearing from the economy.

When I look at these numbers mathematically, I see that there's still $13.3 trillion in economic activity and spending *left* in the economy! To put things in perspective, $13.3 trillion written out as $13,300,000,000,000 has an awful lot of zeros behind it.

When $13.3 trillion in spending is floating around out there, how much of that spending do you need to capture to provide a nice living for your family? The level of spending in a recessionary US economy is still higher than the spending levels of the next four biggest economies in the world combined. More specifically, the US economy, even in its recessionary state, is still larger than the economies of Germany, Japan, China, and the United Kingdom *combined*.

While the actual money being spent in the economy does shrink during a recession, the vast majority of it still remains in the economy. However, the money that stays in the economy is now spent differently from before – serving the new priorities that customers have in a recession that they did not care about previously.

This is why even though economic activity may shrink by 5 percent, in some product categories you'll see spending drop by much larger amounts, such as in new car sales. It's also the reason why in some product and service categories spending actually goes up, such as in car repair services.

This uneven shrinkage of spending across different product categories is actually driven much more by massive shifts in spending priorities among customers than it is by actual reduction in spending in the economy. That is why new car sales can drop by as much as 50 percent in some months even though consumer income and spending has dropped only by, say, 5 percent. It's not that consumers as a group don't have the money, it's that they no longer want to spend it on a new car.

This distinction is important to grasp if you want to survive and prosper in a recession. It's vital to realize that the money is in large part still being spent in the economy. But it's now being spent on different things for different reasons than in previous years.

The analogy I often give to explain this concept is this. Imagine you own a home that's considered prime riverfront property. When you sit outside on your porch, you enjoy this amazing view of the river and watch the river flow by. Now imagine this river isn't made of water, but made of money. For years you sit on the front porch of your home watching the river of money flowing by, picking up your piece of it whenever you care to do so.

But one day, somewhere upstream the river of money gets diverted. It's no longer flowing directly in front of your home. The money is no longer falling into your lap. But, and this is important, the amount of money flowing in that river is still largely out there – it's just flowing somewhere else.

When this happens, you have two choices. The first choice is the choice that most business owners make. They stubbornly sit on their porch staring at the dried-up river bed and wonder, "Where the heck did the river go?"

Then the next day, they come back and do the same thing. They think to themselves, "It's not fair. That river has been flowing in front of my property for years. Where the heck did it go?"

This type of business owner repeats that process of staring at the dry riverbed day in and day out until the business ultimately dies.

The second choice is to get out of the chair on your porch, stop staring at the dry riverbed, and start looking to see where the river of money got diverted to. Remember, most of the money in this river is still out there. But now it's just flowing in a different place than before.

The key to the recession-proof mind-set is to realize that if you want to survive and even prosper, it's up to you to go and find where the money went so you can profit from it.

If your business had a great riverfront location on the river of money in a strong economy but is now positioned in a poor one, it's time to "relocate" or adapt to new market conditions. This is the essence of the recession-proof mind-set.

Mind-Set Tip #2:
Base Business Decisions on Facts, not Headlines

In adopting this recession-proof mind-set, you'll have to be careful about how you let the media influence you. The overwhelming tone of the media is negative. This is for the simple reason that in the media business bad news sells. When markets drop or a key economic indicator falls by even the slightest amount, it becomes instant headline news. The headlines are highly exaggerated all in an effort to get you to tune in.

This happens for two reasons. First, the media industry is going through a tremendous upheaval due to the massive proliferation of alternative news sources. Before the Internet came along, there were only five places you could turn to get major national news: CBS, ABC, NBC, CNN, and your local city paper.

These five news sources had all the news viewership. As the Internet emerged, suddenly there were hundreds of news sites you could get your news from. If you lived in San Francisco, you no longer had to get your news from the *San Francisco Chronicle*; you could get it from the online edition of *The New York Times*, *The Washington Post*, *The Boston Globe*, or any number of newspaper websites.

In addition, with the emergence of blogs you could get wildly different perspectives on the news from quite literally millions of sources. This fragmentation of viewership means that traditional news media receive fewer and fewer viewers and readers. Incidentally, this is why Warren Buffet considers the newspaper business a terrible and dying business.

To stay financially viable, these news organizations have no choice but to follow the "bad news sells" rule of thumb. If CNN doesn't cover the bad news, then MSNBC or CNBC will do it – stealing CNN viewers. The result is an ongoing game of one-upmanship among the media to see which one can turn mildly bad news into the most dramatic, attention-getting headline possible. The kind of headline that shocks you into watching or reading – thereby increasing advertising revenues for the media outlet.

As a frequently called upon expert for the media, having appeared on Fox and MSNBC and in *The Wall Street Journal*, *Inc.* magazine, and *SmartMoney* magazine, I've gotten some insight into this. When media inquiries come to me, they come in waves. It's feast or famine. When I'm asked to serve as an expert for the media, I'll get requests every day for two weeks and then nothing for weeks on end. What happens is one network or magazine picks up a story idea, and then all the other competing media outlets quickly copy it. The entire media industry is driven this way.

Furthermore, the way the media gets its story ideas is very incestuous. They all watch, read, and listen to one another's broadcasts and stories, looking for ideas. The bloggers get blogging ideas from each other. Newspaper reporters get ideas by reading what bloggers write. Television producers get ideas by reading what newspaper reporters write, and the whole incestuous cycle repeats itself.

The problem with this "bad news sells" trend is that it can very seriously skew your interpretation of what's actually going on in the economy and how it might legitimately affect your business.

When hundreds of media sources are taking one tiny bit of bad news and covering it like it's the end of the world, it's very easy to buy into that line of thinking.

Psychologists call this effect the frequency bias. The assumption average human beings make is that the more often they hear a piece of news, the more severe is the problem.

For example, in the United States typically 200 people die from plane crashes each year. Usually that's one crash of a major airliner and a number of crashes of smaller one- to seven-seater aircraft. Whenever such a crash happens, especially of a major airliner, it's splashed all over the news for days. Based on how many stories a person hears, everyone tends to assume that a lot of people die in plane crashes every year.

In contrast, every year in the United States roughly 40,000 people die from car crashes. Factually speaking, car crashes kill nearly 200 times more people than do airplane crashes. Yet because car crashes are so common that news outlets no longer cover them, most people are surprised at the factual differences between these two different types of accidents. Even on a per-mile traveled basis, air travel is much safer.

The moral of this story is simple. Make your business decisions based on facts, not on news stories. Even in a severe recession, there's still a lot of money out there – you just have to go looking for it.

Mind-Set Tip #3:
Exploit the Opportunities that Recessions Create

In advising my clients on how to run their business during challenging economic times, I always tell the following joke. In a recession, your competitors expect to lose business. I suggest that you don't disappoint them!

It's like going to the Olympics when all your competitors are aiming for the bronze medal. It doesn't take *that* much more effort to win gold when everyone else isn't even bothering to try.

One of the big reasons that recessions create opportunities for savvy business owners and CEOs is the massive lack of competition. Your competitors are pulling back, cutting back, hunkering down, and generally waiting passively for the storm to end.

While this is one approach, and even a valid approach if you have tons of cash reserves on hand, it doesn't guarantee survival or success.

When others are hunkering down to ride out the storm, I see an opportunity to get out there and profit from the storm. Go out and sell umbrellas! Or sell sandbags, food rations, fresh water supplies, flashlights, or the many other things that customers really want during a difficult time.

A recession is not the end of the world. It is just a massive shift in priorities and spending patterns. At the end of the day, life still goes on. People still need products and services to continue going about their everyday lives.

People may freeze their spending temporarily in a moment of panic, but eventually they still need to live.

Kids still need to eat breakfast. Businesses still need electricity to run their operations. Life goes on – just a bit differently than before.

The Lance Armstrong Story

Many years ago, I read the biography of Lance Armstrong, seven-time winner of the Tour de France bicycle race. I remember this one story that sort of stuck in my mind. Apparently, in some legs of the Tour de France the riders ride up into the mountains where it gets quite cold.

At certain points in the race, the weather will take a turn for the worse and it will start to rain. What makes this rain especially punishing is that it's in near-freezing temperatures. So the riders are drenched, freezing, and still have to race.

As recounted in the book, during times like these, the riders in the front of the pack would all groan about the miserable conditions.

Guess what Lance Armstrong would do?

When conditions got miserable, he would immediately ride harder and start to sprint ahead of the pack. His logic was simple. He felt he could tolerate misery more than the next guy. And he reasoned that since everyone else was thinking of slowing down, it was precisely the time to speed up, as each surge would get more "bang for the buck," so to speak.

It was precisely at these times that these otherwise aggressive competitors would retaliate and try to keep up or leave him in the dust. But under these miserable conditions, it would break their spirit to see Lance surge ahead. Lance Armstrong is the seven-time winner of the Tour de France for a reason. When others expected to slow down, he opted to speed up.

Flawed Economic Thinking

Most people assume that a recession always means that business gets worse. The assumption is that all businesses are hurt and they are all hurt equally. This is simply not true factually.

In any economy, there are always "winners" and there are always "losers." The competitive nature of our economy is one where the stronger, better-run businesses tend to do better and the ones that are weaker and mismanaged tend to shrink and ultimately go away. This is true regardless of how well or poor the economy in general is doing.

However, it's my point of view that a recession creates many opportunities for the savvy business owner to exploit. Here's why.

Most people see a recession as an overall reduction in customer spending. While this is true, this overly simplified view masks a much more fundamental change, which, if you notice, you can really profit from.

As I mentioned earlier, even though a severe recession might see the economy shrink overall by 5 percent, you're very likely to see spending drop by 50 percent in some categories and spending increase by 10-25 percent in other categories. The overall 5 percent shrinkage is just what happens when you "settle up" all the various changes across the hundreds of sectors of the economy.

It's the underlying *shift* in spending patterns, not the shrinkage in overall spending, that is the key thing to pay attention to. It's these shifts that can kill your business or save it. Forget the overall macro economy numbers; look for where the money is flowing to and position your business to piggyback off it.

The Rules of Success Get Rewritten

This shift in spending completely rewrites the rules of what it takes to be successful in business. While there are some timeless business principles that are always true, you want to position your business to follow the money.

This shift in spending is very disorienting for most business owners. At first it's hard to tell what sectors of the economy are shrinking, holding steady, or even growing modestly. But if you look carefully, you will see these trends emerge. But unlike the loud headlines broadcast by the news, these trends announce themselves with a whisper – loud enough to hear if you're listening for them, but not loud enough to be noticed by someone who expects a recession to be the end of the world.

To illustrate this principle, imagine that you are in a running race. Somewhere in the middle of the race, the race organizers decide to change the rules of the game and turn it into a poker competition. What it takes to be successful in a running race compared to in a poker game is very different. The key to success isn't so much being a good poker player as much as it is *realizing* that the rules of the game have changed and adapting quickly to the new rules.

Mind-Set Tip #4:
Adapt or Die

The key to economic survival and even prosperity is to adapt quickly to new market conditions or risk your business dying. This is, frankly, one of those times where business experience, especially memory of the good times, is a liability.

To make a twist on an old story, there's no sense in crying over spilt milk. Instead, go looking for a new cow!

This theme of "adapt or die" is essential in a recession. While it is possible for many companies to ride out a minor recession, that approach becomes less and less likely to succeed the more severe and longer the recession.

Adaptation is the key to survival.

Speed, Not Size, Matters

When the rules of the game are changing rapidly, being a big company is not always an asset. Speed is the key asset. The ability to adapt to fast-changing circumstances provides security (relatively speaking) for your business.

During times like these, you will see big companies fail for the simple reason that many of them make decisions too slowly or are so bogged down by their physical assets it makes being nimble impossible. The US auto industry comes to mind. It takes five years to take a new product from concept to being available for sale. So even if automakers pick up on change today, it'll be five years before their decisions will be evident in the marketplace.

Similarly, it's not easy to shut down factories and sell them off. Sure, they may sit idle, but the automakers still have to pay loans taken out to finance them.

While physical assets can be a legitimate limitation to making and executing decisions quickly, a slow decision-making process can be lethal in a severe recession.

Decision-Making Cycle Times

Sometimes you find the most useful ideas in the most unusual of places. This is the case when it comes to making business decisions quickly in the midst of a fast-changing economy.

It turns out business owners aren't the only leaders who have the need for fast decision making. In the US military, commanders face the same need during times of war.

I was reading an interesting theory on decision making written by a very insightful former US marine. I forget his name but remember the main idea. If your decision-making cycle time is faster than the enemy's, you have an enormous advantage. The enemy gets confused, can't figure out what to do, reacts to old information, and basically is poised to lose.

Apparently, this is what happened in the deserts during the first Iraq war. Saddam Hussein insisted on making all major military decisions himself. Front-line commanders were not permitted to make major decisions on their own. They had to radio back to headquarters to report new information and to await decisions from Saddam.

So when a tank commander in the Republican Guard saw some US troops somewhere they weren't supposed to be, he would radio back the news and wait to be told what to do. Sometimes it would take an hour or more for headquarters to get back to the Iraqi commander. Of course, by then the rapidly evolving situation had changed and the information used to make the decision was now outdated.

The decision-making process among US field commanders was very different. Clear objectives were given to leaders on the front line. However, those on the front line were encouraged to adapt to rapidly changing battlefield conditions and do whatever was necessary to achieve the overall objective.

So a US tank commander could see a situation develop on the battlefield, assess it, make a decision to adapt, and issue new orders within 20 seconds. Meanwhile, for his counterpart in the Iraqi Republican Guard, the same decision would take minutes or even hours.

US military leaders deliberately kept up the pace of change in the first Iraq war in order to be faster than Iraqi decision-making processes were designed for.

This was one of the reasons why the first Iraq war was won so quickly and decisively.

How to Survive a 100 mph Economic Tornado

When you have a severe tornado bearing down on you at 100 mph, here's a simple survival rule. Get in your car and drive 120 mph in just about any direction, and you'll survive.

In a severe economic "tornado" the same rule applies. In an economic crisis, the rules of the game change so much that the risk of doing nothing is often much higher than doing just about anything else. In other words, if business is lousy, doing nothing ensures that the business dies. But trying to adapt at least gives you a chance of survival. Doing several things to adapt to new conditions ups your odds even more.

The lesson is simple. If your speed of adapting is faster than the speed of change within the economy, you have a good chance of making it. If your speed of adapting is slower than the speed of change within the economy, your business is very much at risk of dying.

In short, remember these two things: 1) adapt or die and 2) speed matters … a lot.

From Mind-Set to Action

Hopefully, through my various stories you can see the value of adopting a recession-proof mind-set. To recap, the key elements to remember are:

1. There's still money out there, but you have to go find it.

2. Base business decisions on facts, not headlines.

3. Exploit the opportunities that recessions create.

4. Adapt or die.

Once you have the right mind-set in place, lets move to Rules #2-#4, which involve making the right decisions.

CHAPTER 2

Rule #2:
Solve a Problem That Gets
Worse in a Recession

In the preface to this book, I mentioned an internal research project that I undertook to look for small businesses that became billion-dollar giants in a recession, depression, or economic panic. This research spanned the last 120 years of US economic history and dozens of interesting case studies.

What's intriguing about the results of this research is the remarkable consistency among these case study companies. All these companies, without exception, had three traits in common – and it's these traits that form the basis of the next three rules to recession-proofing your business formula.

Let's start with the next rule, Rule #2: Solve a Problem That Gets Worse in a Recession.

Guaranteed Customer Demand

Customer demand is not generated. It is merely

channeled. You cannot tell customers to want something they fundamentally do not want. You can try to convince customers to satisfy their demands by buying from you rather than from a competitor. But, ultimately, trying to convince customers that they have a desire when none exists is pointless.

Since customer priorities change in a recession, it's not all that surprising to discover that customer spending patterns change to reflect these new priorities.

While this seems like self-evident common sense, a shockingly high percentage of businesses that were built on the customer spending patterns of a boom economy don't actually change what they offer in a recession.

If what customers spend money on changes in a recession, shouldn't what you offer change right along with it? Similarly, if customers radically change what they spend money on in a recession, shouldn't you at least consider an equally radical change?

One way to guarantee that customer demand will exist for what you have to offer is to provide your customers with a solution to a problem of theirs that gets worse in a recession. When you do this, you guarantee that customer demand exists. Sure, you still have to compete against your competitors to get a piece of that spending, but at least the spending does exist.

This is vital.

It is one thing to compete against a competitor for customer spending that does actually exist. It's another thing entirely to compete for spending that is just not there anymore. The latter will kill your business instantly.

Relevancy Matters

When you look at what you provide to customers, you have to take a hard, critical, emotionally unbiased look at the situation. Do your products and services solve problems that are still relevant to customers during a recession?

If not, you have to change or at a minimum make some adjustments to your product, services, or the marketing used to communicate their relevancy to customers in a recession.

Recession Success Story #1:
Fortune Magazine

Henry Luce launched the first issue of his new magazine concept 90 days after the stock market crash that launched the Great Depression. At the time, his new publication, *Fortune* magazine was expected to fail. It was hard to imagine how a publication that focused exclusively on business issues in great depth could succeed.

The only competitor was *The Wall Street Journal*, which at the time consisted mainly of short articles and a great deal of statistical information about the financial markets. No publication explored the major business issues of the day in any great depth.

However, when the stock market crashed and the 10-year-long Great Depression followed, suddenly the entire country had lost its fortune and was eager for information on how to get it back. *Fortune* piggybacked off this inherent demand to solve a problem that got worse for investors in a recession – finding a way to recover a lost fortune.

Through a combination of insight and a bit of good timing, *Fortune* magazine solved an incredibly relevant problem for its customers during the Great Depression. By the end of the Great Depression, *Fortune* had become mandatory reading for anyone in the United States having anything to do with investment or business. The publication came out of nowhere to dominate the business market – during a depression.

Fortune found the boom marketing within the Great Depression. Even more remarkable is the pricing that Luce was able to charge for the magazine. When the Sunday edition of *The New York Times* cost 5 cents, Luce charged, and got, $1.00 per issue of *Fortune*. That's right, in the midst of the Great Depression he had the guts to charge 20 times more than the highly respected Sunday edition of *The New York Times*.

While Luce certainly had the guts, he also had the "wind at his back" by solving a problem that gets worse for customers during a recession. When you do this you not only increase your ability to grow unit sales but also do it at a premium price – providing superior profit margins in a recession.

Recession Success Story #2:
Federal Express

At the height of the oil crisis in 1973, with jet fuel prices at sky-high levels, Federal Express launched its trademark overnight delivery service. How in the world does a company charge 20 times more than its nearest competitor; have its primary costs, jet fuel, triple in price; and still become a Fortune 500 company?

This is the infrequently told story of Fred Smith and Federal Express. Fred Smith was a college student at Yale University and a private pilot. He loved to fly planes and spent a lot of time at the local commuter airport in New Haven, Connecticut.

In the late 1960s, he noticed that a number of the small four-seater passenger aircraft flying in and out of his home airport flew **without** passengers. He thought this was odd. Curious, he began hanging out in the pilots' bar to find an answer to this unusual phenomenon.

It turned out that most of these pilots were flying charter flights for IBM and Xerox, both of which had major centers of operation in the area. But instead of flying IBM and Xerox executives, these planes had been chartered to fly spare parts for mainframe computers sold by IBM and Xerox to their Fortune 500 clients.

Fred Smith thought it was terribly inefficient to charter an entire plane just to fly a 2-ounce computer chip across the country. But IBM and Xerox's Fortune 500 clients demanded it.

You see, as the oil crisis started, the big companies laid off a number of employees. This is so common these days it's hardly news. During the recession, these big companies had a big and growing problem. The work that needed to be done was growing, even though their staff levels were shrinking. IBM and Xerox solved their

---

clients' problems by providing computer technology to automate much of the work previously done by people.

The only problem was the computer systems provided by IBM and Xerox would break down and need to be repaired. IBM and Xerox service contracts guaranteed that in the event their computer systems failed, they would fix the equipment absolutely, positively by the next business day. Does this sound familiar?

Fred Smith noticed this trend and saw the problem get worse as the US economy headed into a recession. He launched Federal Express as an overnight computer spare parts delivery service primarily for companies like IBM and Xerox. While his prices per pound were 20 times higher than those of the US Postal Service, he astutely pointed out to IBM and Xerox that his shipping prices were 99 percent less expensive than chartering an entire plane!

Fred Smith turned Federal Express into a Fortune 500 company by serving a need that got worse in a recession – the need for rapid delivery of spare computer parts necessary to run the computers of Fortune 500 companies that used technology to do the work of employees they had laid off.

And why did Fred Smith decide that FedEx's slogan would be "When it absolutely, positively has to be there the next day"? Because IBM and Xerox refused to do business with FedEx unless those demands could be met.

While many credit Fred Smith with being an inventive business genius, we should really be crediting Fred Smith for being observant and being a good listener. When you bother to look for the problems that get worse in a recession, you will spot them. When you understand the underlying dynamics behind these problems, opportunities suddenly become visible.

It's a Matter of Perspective

Fred Smith had amazing insight into his customers' problems. But if you think about it, the key pieces of information that led to the formation of Federal Express were "hiding" in plain sight for anyone to see.

- Observation #1: In a recession, big companies lay off employees.

- Observation #2: Big companies use computers to automate work that laid-off employees used to do.

- Observation #3: Computers break down and need to be repaired.

- Observation #4: Customers of big companies get angry when those companies' computers are down, resulting in poor customer service, late shipments, and defective products.

These four observations are hardly big secrets. All of them are common sense. But only Fred Smith was able to see the big picture and piece together what was under the noses of everyone in the country.

And because he had the right mind-set (going back to Rule #1 again), he looked for problems to solve, took the time to understand his customers' problems (and you could argue their customers' problems too), and found a way to solve them.

The result was that Federal Express was able to ride a huge wave of increasing customer demand in the midst of a major recession, an oil crisis, and runaway inflation.

When you take the time to find and solve a problem that gets worse in a recession, it gives you customer demand – one of the key assets you need to create a recession-proof business.

CHAPTER 3

Rule #3:
Make Your Business
Competition-Proof

While ensuring customer demand is necessary to create a recession-proof business, by itself it's not enough. There is still the competition factor. When you have strong customer demand but even stronger competition it's still possible to lose.

So the next step in the recession-proof business formula is to make your business competition-proof by marginalizing or making your competitors irrelevant to your customers.

Here's how to do this.

Once you've found a problem that gets worse for customers during a recession, solve that problem in a *unique* way — this is the key to making a business competition-proof or at least partially insulated from the actions of competitors. This uniqueness factor is very important. When you're able to offer a unique product or service that solves an escalating problem for customers, you are able to connect increasing demand with limited supply. In short, you create a "mini" monopoly.

This is the ideal position to be in during a recession: strong customer demand with little to no competition. Offering something unique to the marketplace is the key to marginalizing your competition.

The Blue Ocean – Beyond Market Differentiation

At first glance, this rule for recession-proofing your business seems to suggest that market differentiation is important. But, as you'll see from the following examples, to really recession-proof your business you need to go well beyond modest market differentiation.

The best book on this topic is called *Blue Ocean Strategy* by INSEAD business school professors W. Chan Kim and Renée Mauborgne. In my opinion, *Blue Ocean Strategy* is one of the two best books ever written on the topic of strategy (the other being *Competitive Strategy* by Michael Porter).

I'm not often a fan of books written by ivory tower business school professors who have never had profit and loss responsibility. The ideas are usually interesting but not always practical. However, *Blue Ocean Strategy* is remarkably insightful and practical.

For me, this is very big praise. The two compliments that I value the most, both in giving to others and in receiving myself, are "insightful" and "practical." An idea, concept, or tool is insightful when it is factually supported but not always obvious. In the world of ideas, it gives you an edge in leading your business in a direction that you might not otherwise have taken without this "insight." Usually an insightful idea, once understood, is powerful in its simplicity and jibes with common sense. But often this perspective isn't achieved until someone has explained the insight – unlocking one's appreciation for the idea.

An idea is practical if it's useful in the real world and can make numbers move on the profit and loss statement. Thus a great idea is one that gives you an edge, especially one that you wouldn't have noticed on your own, and is useful in the real world. The ideas in *Blue Ocean Strategy* pass both these tests. They are both insightful and useful.

Let me explain the concept behind *Blue Ocean Strategy* so you will notice how companies like the Coors Brewing Company and Price Club (now known as Costco) used it to create new markets that dominated.

Blue Ocean Strategy argues that there are two types of markets. One market is characterized by many competitors all trying to do essentially the same thing. These companies bloody each other in trying to compete for the same customers in the same way. And by doing so, they bloody the waters, creating a "red ocean."

While these companies do their best to differentiate their products and services, the range of differentiation is quite narrow. An example of this would be the many e-commerce websites that sell music CDs via the Internet. All these competitors offer the same selection and shipping options, essentially only competing on price – again bloodying the waters in that market.

In contrast, a blue ocean is created when a company goes off in a radically different direction. In essence, it finds a "blue ocean" that is completely absent of competition. This usually involves finding an underserved customer segment to focus on, creating a product/service combination that's radically different from pre-existing options, or doing both.

An example of a company creating a blue ocean would be Apple's wildly successful iPod and iTunes combination. Steve Jobs at Apple correctly realized that consumers did not want music CDs, they just wanted music, period. Apple came up with the iPod portable digital music player that allowed thousands of songs to be stored digitally so that you could take your entire music library with you on the go.

Next, they created the iTunes online music download service. Instead of being forced to buy an entire CD that may only contain one song that you really want, iTunes made it possible to buy just the one song you really wanted. They also developed a new digital rights management system that would prevent piracy – a key obstacle that had earlier prevented major music labels from selling music this way.

The combination of a cool-looking portable music player, a digital download music service, and the piracy protection assurance that attracted music labels in droves, created a radically different approach to providing music to consumers. Within months, Apple acquired 60-80 percent market share in the online music industry and has held it ever since.

While Apple pulled off its blue ocean strategy during a boom economy, the approach is equally effective in an economic recession or depression.

Recession Success Story #3:
The Coors Brewing Company

In 1873, Adolph Coors, a 26-year-old immigrant from Prussia, decided to start a brewing company. This was the same year that the longest economic depression in US history began. It would last 20 years – double the length of the Great Depression.

Coors was an observant young entrepreneur. He noticed that in the midst of an economic crisis, people get depressed. And what do people do when they're depressed? Well ... they drink alcohol.

While this may not be the most productive thing to do in a depression, it is nonetheless what many people choose to do. Coors noticed this and capitalized on this demand by starting the Coors Brewing Company.

While Coors followed our earlier rule about solving a problem that gets worse in a recession – in this case the need for alcohol – he did this in a radically different way than his competitors.

At the time, most of the population in the United States was in the eastern half of the country. Not surprisingly, most of the major brewing companies were located near these population centers.

At the same time, the US population was slowly migrating westward. But the transportation infrastructure in the western settlements and towns was nowhere near as well established as in the cities back east. This made logistics, shipping, and delivery problematic for any company doing business out west. All the major breweries in the East largely ignored the beer-thirsty customers out west. The population was spread out, the terrain was rough, and the support infrastructure was not there. Operating costs and headaches were bound to be high.

But Adolph Coors had a different idea. While he had apprenticed as a brewmaster in his home country of Prussia and in numerous US breweries in the East, when it came time to leave his own mark and set up shop he decided to "zig" when everyone else "zagged."

He set up his brewery in Golden, Colorado, in the Rocky Mountains. In his sales and marketing plan, he targeted two distinct markets: those consumers living in the settlements scattered across the western United States and the miners that were working new mining operations in the same area.

In both cases, these thirsty consumers didn't have many choices when it came to beer. Coors was the only brewer willing to establish a far-flung transportation infrastructure to get his beer delivered to remote parts of the western United States.

While his product was good, it wasn't necessarily that much better than the beer from other breweries. What made the Coors Brewing Company unique was its geographic focus and the sophisticated distribution infrastructure it built to serve the customers in these areas.

Adolph Coors found himself a blue ocean and found that Coors Brewing Company had a mini-monopoly for decades. Today the company, now known as the Molson Coors Brewing Company, generates $7 billion a year in sales. It all started by building a small business that was radically different in its focus – insulating itself from competitors for many years. It positioned Coors to prosper in a 20-year depression – one that was double the duration of the Great Depression.

Recession Success Story #4: Price Club

In 1976, Sol Price started Price Club and pioneered the wholesale warehouse club business. Years later, Price Club would merge with Costco (started by one of Sol Price's protégés) and take on the Costco name. Today, it is a $70 billion a year retail business.

Price Club was started in between two back-to-back recessions. The two-year-long oil crisis and stock market crash that began in 1973 in part inspired the Price Club concept, but it was during the 1980 oil crisis and recession that Price Club's growth began to kick in.

Sol Price noticed during the first recession that small-business owners were struggling to compete against their larger competitors that had more buying power. Customers were spending less, but owners of small businesses were not able to press their suppliers to cut their prices. Sol Price spotted a problem that he thought he could solve.

His idea was to create a wholesale business targeted toward small businesses. He would be the middleman who got small business real wholesale pricing on everything from office supplies, food, and paper products to tires and more.

But more than just buying in bulk and selling at lower prices, Price took a much more radical approach. Instead of selling the quantities his customers wanted, he forced them to buy in much larger quantities than they were accustomed to or could immediately use. He did this to get greater negotiating power among his suppliers.

In other words, in exchange for incredibly low pricing, he created a problem for customers – huge quantities of stuff they would have to find some way to store.

It turns out that this tradeoff was one that many customers were willing to make. These customers included my parents.

You see, I grew up in San Diego, and we used to shop at the first Price Club warehouse that Sol Price opened. My parents owned their own small business and used to buy everything from coffee, paper towels, and packing tape to countless things they needed for their office. We also ended up buying food and supplies for personal use.

When I say that Price Club created a problem for its customers, I know from firsthand experience. Being the oldest son, I was the one who had to load the 100 rolls of toilet paper, 100 pounds of photocopy paper, and the countless other heavy and bulky items my mom would purchase. My younger brother got off scot-free, saying, "Mom, the Price Club stuff is taller, wider, and heavier than me!" It's tough to argue with that one.

This giving you more than you really could use was a real problem. All the stuff wouldn't fit into the small sedan my mom drove. So when the time came to get a new car, she decided to try one of those new minivans that were just becoming popular – all so we could fit everything she wanted to buy at Price Club into the car in only one trip.

In my parents' place of business, they carved out a special part of the office to store all these things they bought at Costco. They put in new shelves and cabinets to store all this extra stuff.

At home, I had to reorganize the garage to make room for the 100-day supply we had of everything. My toys were out, Price Club stuff was in. A very memorable experience for a kid, I can tell you.

Price Club radically redefined the value equation provided to customers. It didn't offer exactly what you wanted at the lowest possible price. It offered you way more than you needed at prices way lower than you thought possible. It was the definition of radical differentiation.

Market Domination

In the nine years that followed the formation of Price Club, the warehouse store business grew to a $2 billion per year industry. Price Club generated $1.8 billion of those sales for a commanding 90 percent market share.

This growth was not lost on another well-known retailer, Sam Walton, the founder of Wal-Mart. He noticed this little San Diego company leading the fastest-growing portion of the retail industry and decided to compete.

Taking the Wal-Mart threat seriously, Sol Price, who commanded the #1 market share Price Club, decided to merge with Costco, the #3 market share player, in 1993. The merged company took on the Costco name and today generates $70 billion a year in sales. It is #29 on the list of Fortune 500 companies.

To this day, Costco dominates its industry, and remarkably its original formula of "too much" product for absurdly low prices remains largely unchanged. This is just one powerful consequence of offering something unique to your marketplace.

Uniqueness Increases Profit Margins and Sales Simultaneously

But the Price Club/Costco story gets better. Even more impressive than how Price Club's sales accelerated during recessions is the fact that the company does virtually no advertising. Think about it. When was the last time you saw any kind of advertising for the company now known as Costco? Except for a few flyers handed out to customers on their way into or out of a Costco warehouse, the company doesn't do any advertising.

That's incredible: $70 billion in sales and virtually no advertising or marketing.

How is this possible?

Again, it goes back to offering something really unique (and relevant) to customers. When you astound customers with how unique your offerings are, they do your marketing for you.

When I was a kid, we would routinely have relatives come visit us from overseas. Invariably, we would take our relatives to visit Disneyland and then we'd take them to Price Club. When we told them of our plans, they thought it was bizarre. "You want to take us to some big industrial warehouse to go shopping? Huh, how does that work?"

We were so enthusiastic about Price Club, we just had to show them what it was all about. And perhaps that sounds a bit crazy, but even more crazy was that my overseas relatives loved it. They would step into Price Club and see it was just enormous. They had never seen anything like it. Then they looked at how everything was packaged. Instead of buying 1 pound of sugar at a time like they were used to, we would buy 25 pounds of sugar for the same price they paid to buy 3 pounds. It blew their minds away that such a thing was possible.

But a funny thing happened; when my relatives flew home, they told my other overseas relatives about their trip. So when my other relatives came on trips, they too wanted to go see this Price Club thing. It was as big a deal as Disneyland because it was really unique. In addition to spreading the Price Club story to our relatives, I spread the word to neighbors, friends from school, and casual acquaintances. My parents' employees saw the 30-pound bags of coffee beans and the 200 rolls of toilet paper and quickly figured out where it came from and ultimately became Price Club customers too.

When you offer something radically different to your customers (and assuming it's incredibly relevant to their needs in a recession), they can't help but tell their friends about it.

I've been talking about Price Club for nearly 30 years to anyone who will listen. I'm even writing about it in this book! Needless to say, if it wasn't unique, none of that would ever have happened.

Now let me translate what all this means in financial terms. When you offer something unique to your market, the "cost of sales and marketing" portion of your profit and loss statement drops like a rock. This improves your profit margin percentages (the profit made per every $100 in sales), which is especially nice in a recession. Next, because your customers are talking about your business to their friends and acquaintances, they are driving new customer acquisition and top line sales. So it's like getting a bigger slice of the pie as profit and getting more pies at the same time. It's a double benefit.

From an accountant or chief financial officer's perspective, this is the best of both worlds – increasing unit sales and profit margins during a recession. Again, being unique – while still being relevant – is what makes the difference.

In a subsequent chapter I'll walk you through a systematic process for figuring out how to be unique in your marketplace. For now, just recognize the importance this plays in recession-proofing your business.

CHAPTER 4

Rule #4:
Market More Aggressively,
Not Less

When I first learned to drive a car, my driving instructor told me to turn the steering wheel in the direction I wanted to head *before* I stepped on the gas pedal. In other words, be sure of your navigation before you accelerate.

The four rules to creating a recession-proof business follow the same logic. Rule #2 (Solve a Problem That Gets Worse in a Recession) and Rule #3 (Make Your Business Competition-proof) are both designed to help you navigate your business more effectively. These two rules allow you to plot your company's direction to pick up customer demand while minimizing competition.

In Fortune 500, they call this "strategy" or "strategic planning." I personally don't like the term "strategy" because while the average business owner has heard of the word, most don't have much of a strategy. I think it's because even though people know the word, they don't appreciate its meaning.

Instead of strategy, I prefer the term "navigation." Imagine you are the captain of your own ship (or business). You see a huge storm coming over the horizon on one side. You see jagged cliffs on the other. Navigation is all about how you're going to steer the ship to survive. Do you turn into the storm? Or turn toward the rock? Do you speed up? Or do you slow down?

A good navigator will give guidance to the captain, in this case you, on how to plot the course. The navigator recommends specific direction changes, the sequence of those changes, and their timing to reach the desired destination or outcome.

Remember the Titanic? It was a great ship, with a great crew, but with terrible navigation. You make the wrong decisions about direction, and it is life threatening for a boat and certainly for a business.

In the early stages of working with clients on a one-on-one basis, most of my work as an executive coach relates to navigation issues. Fundamentally, is the boat pointed in the wrong direction? If it's not, what's the fastest, least risky, cheapest way to get the ship pointing in the right direction?

But once the fundamental direction is set, the focus shifts to speed of execution, or stepping on the gas pedal. How quickly can you improve the operations on the ship to pick up the pace and reach your destination faster? I think of this as operations, or the execution of the navigation plan.

This is critical. If you don't have good navigation, efficient operation is pointless. Imagine that the crew of the Titanic could run the engines faster than any other ship in the Atlantic. When you have poor navigation, great execution only sends the boat faster toward an untimely demise. In other words, when your navigation has you pointed toward a lethal iceberg, speed of execution is *not* an asset.

Phrased differently, navigation is the steering wheel. The gas pedal is execution. Don't put the pedal to the metal if you don't know where you're going!

I'm attempting to illustrate the subtleties of this concept in several different ways for a reason. It's vital not just to be aware of these ideas but to really grasp and master them. Here's why.

In a challenging economy, most CEOs and business owners instinctively slow down and hunker down. Much like you and I will ease off the gas pedal when we roll into a bank of fog. We slow down to be more cautious and in some cases stop entirely to wait the fog out. Typically this instinct serves us well.

But as it applies to business, we have these issues of overhead and cash flow. Every minute not moving at full speed is extremely expensive. Depending on how well capitalized your business is or the size of your cash reserves, you may not be able to slow down or stop doing business indefinitely. Most businesses can afford to slow down temporarily, but most cannot stop doing business entirely or they'll simply run out of "gas" or cash, as the case may be.

That is why the first three rules of the recession-proof business formula are so vital. Rule #1 about adopting a recession-proof mind-set prompts you to base your business "navigation" decisions by looking at the facts, not the news headlines. Much like how an experienced pilot can fly through fog by looking at the instruments (the facts) and ignoring the tricks the eyes can play on someone when looking out the window (or looking at the TV, as the case may be).

Rules #2 and #3 about solving a problem that gets worse in a recession and finding a way to insulate yourself from competition plots the navigation course to keep moving toward your destination without running into life-threatening obstacles.

Once you have these elements in place – great clarity about the pros and cons of your situation and a clear path to navigate – it makes sense to speed up your rate of execution. The part of your business that sets the tempo for the whole company is your sales and marketing efforts.

When the first three rules of the recession-proofing formula have been followed, the next rule to follow is to be *more* aggressive in your sales and marketing efforts – not less.

At first glance, this seems contrary to "conventional wisdom." Conventional wisdom, which is the wisdom of the average person, suggests you should hunker down and lie low in a recession. Cut back on everything. Cut back on sales, cut back on marketing, cut back on research and development, cut back on service. Hunker down. Wait for the storm to blow over.

If you don't have a business that's well positioned to take advantage of opportunities created by a recession, hunkering down or shutting down your business are really the only viable options.

But if your business is well positioned, it makes much more sense to be more aggressive in your sales and marketing efforts. This is the case for several reasons.

First, what you have to offer is actually beneficial to customers in a recession. But in many cases they don't know about what you have to offer. In other cases they may not fully appreciate or understand how what you offer is relevant to their needs in a recession.

A more aggressive sales and marketing effort enables you to communicate with customers and help them "connect the dots" between what they care about and what you have to offer. Don't expect customers to connect the dots themselves; that's your company's job.

Second, when your competitors are hunkering down and hiding from buyers, it doesn't take that much effort to stand out. It's like when someone says, "Will the person who runs the best company for me to buy from please stand up" and the CEOs of all your competitors promptly sit down, and you win. In other words, as the competition fades away, it becomes easier and easier to get customers – provided you're even bothering to try.

Recession Success Story #5:
United Parcel Service (UPS)

In 1907, the United States was in the midst of an economic panic with unusually high unemployment. For the unemployed who were looking to do something to make money, many were willing to take more risks. Better to have a shot at a better life than to sit still with no income.

At that time gold had been discovered in remote parts of Alaska. This gold rush turned Seattle into a boomtown, as it was the closest major city that many gold seekers used as a staging area to get to Alaska.

As Seattle boomed and became a commerce hub, getting packages and messages delivered became an increasingly challenging problem. The messenger services that existed at the time were notoriously unreliable and were shady in some cases.

This was the economic situation that 19-year-old James Casey grew up with. He saw a strong, growing demand for messenger and package delivery services even in the midst of an economic panic. He also noticed a gap in the marketplace—an underserved need that he thought he could use to create a unique business. What was this underserved need? In a word: reliability.

So James Casey started a messenger and package delivery service known as United Parcel Service. He knew that there was demand for this service – following one of the keys to creating a recession-proof business. He also decided to offer an impeccably reliable delivery service – which was at the time radically different from the competition. By doing so, he followed the other key to creating a recession-proof business – solving customers' problems in a unique way.

But he intuitively knew that alone was not enough. Sure, he had customer demand for his industry. Yes, he offered a unique approach to solving his clients' problems. But he had one problem – none of his prospective customers knew about the unique reliability that UPS had to offer.

Casey recognized this reality and put as much effort into marketing his unique service as he did in managing the day-to-day operations of the service itself. In fact, he blended these two efforts so seamlessly it's hard to distinguish which decision was a client service decision and which was a marketing one.

Here's the story of how UPS got off the ground.

Casey knew from the outset that reliability would be not only the key to differentiating his service but also the cornerstone of his marketing efforts. He realized that reliability was not a physical attribute like color, weight, or size. It was an intangible quality about his service that was not visible to the human eye. So his marketing was quite clever in finding visual and auditory cues to communicate this intangible quality of reliability.

He started by hiring the "good kids" from his high school. As a kid himself, he knew which kids were responsible and which kids got into trouble. He cherry-picked the most responsible teenagers he could find.

Next, he made every one of his employees wear the exact same uniform. While the uniforms weren't the brown color we're used to today, they consisted of a nice shirt and a matching baseball cap. He trained his staff to be exceptionally polite with customers and made sure they showed up on time. He was insistent on this.

He figured that if his employees all dressed the same, behaved in the same polite manner, and showed up on time every single time, his customers would believe his promise of having a reliable service.

Next, he painted his three bicycles and two cars all the same color. Originally, that color was supposed to be yellow. But at the last minute, Casey's business partner convinced him that dirt on yellow-painted bicycles and cars would stand out more – ruining the reliable message he was trying to convey. As an alternative, Casey's partner suggested brown. The decision was approved and all delivery vehicles were promptly painted brown.

But the one decision that really put Casey over the top was his decision to be open for business 24 hours a day, 7 days a week, 365 days a year – far from the norm in 1907. Casey was a lifelong bachelor. He never married and never had kids. UPS was his life.

He and his business partner both put cots in the UPS offices, and they actually lived and slept there every single day. To make his point about reliability, he encouraged customers to call UPS at 2 a.m. on Christmas Day – because when you call we will be there. Call at midnight on Thanksgiving Day – no problem, because we're UPS and we'll be there.

He drilled this message into the minds of his active and prospective clients over and over again. He backed up this message with operational execution that delivered on the promise. Phone calls at 2 a.m. really were answered. Package pickups were always on time. Packages were delivered when they were supposed to be.

The combination of offering something unique to customers and aggressively marketing this uniqueness launched UPS.

What I find so remarkable about the UPS story is that James Casey's unique formula for UPS in 1907 remains largely unchanged more than 100 years later. Think about why people use UPS today. I know I use it because, well, the stuff I ship with them gets there. I use UPS because it's reliable.

It's amazing that a business founded 100 years ago, one based on the unique idea of providing an exceptionally reliable package delivery service, still exists, still dominates, and is used by customers today for pretty much the same reasons that customers used it 100 years ago. Amazing.

Sales and Marketing Execution

The role of marketing in a recession is so vital to recession-proofing your business that I've devoted an entire section of the book to the topic.

For now, it's useful to appreciate the importance of marketing in recession-proofing your business. And it's equally useful to keep in mind the prerequisite conditions needed to feel comfortable about marketing more aggressively, namely solving a problem that customers still care about in a recession and solving that problem in a unique way. When you have these two elements in place, marketing more aggressively is the right move. We'll cover this in much more detail shortly.

CHAPTER 5

More Recession
Success Stories

So far, I've outlined the four major rules of the recession-proof business formula:

- Rule #1: Adopt the Recession-proof Mind-set

- Rule #2: Solve a Problem That Gets Worse in a Recession

- Rule #3: Make Your Business Competition-proof

- Rule #4: Market More Aggressively, Not Less

In this chapter, I'll share several other recession success stories. You'll see how these small-businesses-turned-billion–dollar-giants all followed these four rules in their own way.

You'll find example after example of companies that were inspired by and later exploited trends that emerged in a recession.

Recession Success Story #6:
The Walt Disney Company

In 1928, Walt and Roy Disney started The Walt Disney Company. In that year, they released a cartoon film *Steamboat Willie* – the first Mickey Mouse cartoon feature with sound. While the Disney brothers' company was off to a successful first 11 months of operations, in the 12th month it ran straight into the Great Depression.

While you might think that a cartoon company would struggle in an economy where people could only afford the essentials, the opposite proved to be true – at least for Disney.

Historically, entertainment is a recession-resistant industry. When a recession hits, the impact on entertainment is usually delayed. This happens because the demand for escapism from the recession goes up. People get burnt out by all the negativity from a recession and simply need a break. Vacations become difficult to afford, so entertainment often fills that need.

However, the Great Depression was so severe that industrywide box office sales were down. So even though all the companies in the entertainment industry followed Rule #2: Solve a Problem That Gets Worse in a Recession, most suffered because while the need for entertainment went up, it was offset by the lack of discretionary income.

Unlike its competitors, The Walt Disney Company had a unique approach to entertaining its customers (following Rule #3: Make Your Business Competition-proof). The two key things that differentiated Disney during this time were its amazing cartoon characters and cutting-edge usage of audio sound in its cartoon films. These two innovations set Disney apart from the competition quite literally from day one. These differences allowed Disney to "steal" customers from its competitors that had nothing unique to offer this quickly shrinking market.

The result was that Disney actually grew and prospered during the Great Depression. The more that people were depressed by the economic news, the more they went to watch (and listen to) Disney films. Word of mouth spread about the amazing animation and soundtracks in Disney cartoon films, allowing Disney to expand its marketing reach (Rule #4) while also using the uniqueness of its product to lower the costs of sales and marketing.

The combination of these factors allowed Disney to survive and prosper in the Great Depression when most of its competitors failed.

Recession Success Story #7:
Hewlett-Packard

In 1935, two aspiring young engineers who had graduated from Stanford University looked to set their market. The Great Depression had been in full swing for six years and opportunities seemed scarce. Bill Hewlett and David Packard saw the emerging importance of electronic test equipment used in many aspects of industry. With an investment of $538, the pair launched a company to take advantage of this emerging market.

Their first product was an audio oscillator used to test audio equipment in the emerging market for audio sound. In fact, one of Hewlett-Packard's first customers was another recession success story company, The Walt Disney Company.

Walt Disney with its first audio cartoon, *Steamboat Willie*, had proven the incredible consumer appeal of sound and the relative financial safety it provided to the company.

Disney quickly moved to incorporate sound into all of its film projects and soon had a ton of audio equipment that had to be tested, validated, and calibrated to ensure that it worked properly. Audio equipment was not only used in the recording of films but was also used in displaying them. Hundreds, if not thousands, of movie theaters across the country had to have audio equipment installed and then tested to verify sound fidelity and volume level consistency.

Since the audio equipment was relatively new, the support electronics to maintain this equipment was an emerging market – even during the Great Depression. Hewlett-Packard's superior engineering skills found a different, radically less expensive method to create an audio oscillator. This technological uniqueness allowed HP to sell its products at a unique price point. Even though HP prices were 75 percent less than its competitors' prices, it was able to maintain healthy profit margins.

HP piggybacked off the growing demand to support, maintain, and calibrate electronic devices. It served that need in a uniquely engineered way that gave it an enormous advantage. The combination made HP recession proof.

Recession Success Story #8:
Domino's Pizza

In 1960, two brothers by the name of Tom and James Monaghan opened a pizza shop to serve the students of Eastern Michigan University. Within the first eight months of starting the business, James Monaghan wanted out of the business. The country was in the midst of a recession and James thought the chances of the business succeeding were slim.

Tom Monaghan thought differently. He figured that even in a recession college kids still have to eat. So Tom bought his brother's half of the business in exchange for a used Volkswagen Beetle. Both brothers were thrilled.

Tom Monaghan's pizza business survived the recession and he spent the next several years mastering two unique aspects of the Domino's pizza business – pizza delivery and franchising.

Most pizza restaurants at the time were sit-down restaurants. Monaghan thought that turning the restaurant business into a food delivery business was unique. He was right.

In the years that followed, he perfected the operational aspects of the pizza making and delivery business. He got his operations down cold so that his stores were able to deliver a pizza usually within 30 minutes. This was an attractive benefit for the hungry "gotta eat now" college crowd that the early Domino's locations tended to serve.

At the same time, he slowly began to acquire franchisees to harness their capital and sweat equity to open more locations.

By the time the 1973 oil crisis and recession hit, Monaghan was ready to make his big move. At the start of the economic crisis, Domino's announced its now famous guarantee, "Hot, fresh pizza in 30 minutes or less ... or it's free!"

Domino's would keep this unique guarantee for a full 20 years before ultimately canceling it because of rising concerns and legal costs due to drivers speeding and injuring people during their deliveries.

But what's interesting about this 20-year period is that the company's sales skyrocketed. The company grew from a handful of franchisees to more than a thousand. While Domino's spawned a number of competing pizza delivery places, no other company ever had the operational skills, the franchise base, or the guts to offer and deliver on such a unique promise. This simple concept of getting your pizza in 30 minutes or less or it's free went unmatched by any other competitor for two decades.

Why did Domino's survive and actually thrive during multiple recessions?

It served a never-ending need – hunger (following Rule #2: Solve a Problem That Gets Worse in a Recession). It provided a unique, fast pizza delivery solution to the "I'm hungry now" problem (following Rule #3: Make Your Business Competition-proof). Finally, it marketed its uniqueness in the most gutsy and aggressive of ways with its "Hot, fresh pizza in 30 minutes or less ... or it's free" guarantee.

Tom Monaghan made Domino's Pizza recession-proof by following all the rules of the recession-proof business formula. In 1998, he sold the company for more than a billion dollars – of which half came from his brother James's original share of the business. Sometimes a good plan with the courage to see it through when others are scared pays off in the end. It sure did for Tom Monaghan.

Recession Success Story #9:
Charles Schwab

In 1971, Charles Schwab started his first company, First Commander Corp., to create a stock mutual fund. While the young company quickly acquired $20 million in client money to manage, Schwab ran into problems with government regulators. Unaware of the financial security laws, Schwab had inadvertently violated a number of them by failing to register his mutual with the proper government agencies. The US government promptly forced Schwab's company out of business.

Licking his wounds, Schwab realized his mistake and decided to pay attention to these laws and how they limit or create business opportunities in the world of finance. This hard-learned lesson would stay with him when he opened the company he is now famous for, Charles Schwab & Co., Inc.

The year was 1974, the US stock market had crashed the year before, oil prices had skyrocketed nearly 400 percent, and economic growth was nowhere to be found. This was hardly the ideal time to start a company in the financial sector, but Schwab did so nonetheless. Originally, Charles Schwab & Co., Inc., was intended to be a money management firm where Schwab himself would manage his clients' money for them. It was supposed to be a legal version of his original First Commander Corp.

In 1975, with the country still in the midst of a recession, the US government passed a law that would deregulate the stock brokerage industry. Up until that time, the New York Stock Exchange had set the specific commission price that its brokerage firm members were allowed to charge. In other words, brokers like Merrill Lynch and its competitors didn't set commission rates; they all charged the commission rates predetermined by the New York Stock Exchange.

When the price they were required to charge couldn't be changed up or down, it forced the major brokerage firms to compete on providing more services to clients. This led all the major firms to start investment research divisions that would provide better buy/sell recommendations to clients. The thought was that if you could buy or sell any stock through any brokerage firm for the same price, clients were likely to favor those firms that provided the most comprehensive research for free.

When this new deregulation law was passed, brokerage firms were no longer required to set their prices based on what the New York Stock Exchange requested. They were free to do whatever they pleased.

Initially, all the major firms did nothing. Their business models were working just fine and they were reluctant to rock the boat and make any major changes.

A young Charles Schwab, who had learned his lesson about ignoring the laws regulating finance, studied the new law and the opportunities that might come with it.

The first conclusion he reached was that the brokerage business could now be a much more price-competitive business. While he thought about starting a lower-priced brokerage company, he could not figure out how to lower the operating costs of the business. Merrill Lynch had a huge presence. It had lots of brokers and many research analysts. Schwab could not figure out how he could provide the same or higher quality research for less money than Merrill Lynch could.

He quickly realized that beating Merrill Lynch at its own game was impossible. Merrill Lynch was huge. The cost of a Merrill Lynch analyst coming up with a single buy or sell recommendation could be spread out across millions of clients. For Schwab to match the Merrill Lynch cost efficiency in research, he'd have to start his brokerage business with millions of clients on the first day – clearly not realistic.

So he decided that since he couldn't possibly beat Merrill Lynch at its own game, he would play an entirely different game. He decided to provide no research whatsoever to his clients.

This was a radical departure from what was the industry norm. But Schwab studied the laws carefully and realized that the practice, although different, was perfectly legal.

While Merrill Lynch had to charge high fees to pay for its very expensive research team, Schwab had no research team at all and could pass along the savings to his customers. Thus the first major discount stock brokerage was created.

Today the idea doesn't seem all that radical. But at the time it sent shock waves through the industry. It was the total opposite of what everybody in the industry thought the brokerage business was about – research. Even Schwab himself was originally in the research business by managing other people's money (through research) with First Commander Corp. and the original plan for Charles Schwab & Co., Inc.

But when these new laws were passed, Schwab was willing to ditch conventional wisdom and to essentially throw away a career's worth of stock research skills to offer investors something radically different.

Schwab clearly had followed Rule #3 of competition-proofing your business by offering something unique. At the same time, US investors were still reeling from their losses from a major stock market crash. Those investors that had followed Merrill Lynch research advice lost just as much money as those who didn't.

A segment of investors decided that research from the major brokerage firms did not make a big difference in their financial returns. These investors decided to do their own homework on stocks and started to wonder why they were still paying, through higher fees, for research they never used. As the recession continued, the trend of investors feeling alienated by research advice from the major firms grew.

This fast-growing group of investors would make up Charles Schwab's initial group of customers – and they flocked to Schwab in droves. This trend allowed Schwab to follow Rule #2: Solve a Problem That Gets Worse in a Recession. This fast-growing group of dissatisfied investors had nowhere to turn to – until the Charles Schwab & Co., Inc., discount brokerage appeared.

Despite the recession, Schwab knew he had something unique to offer so he aggressively increased his sales, marketing, and expansion efforts – following Rule #4 of being more aggressive, rather than less, in a recession.

He opened small offices in major cities across the country – usually right next door to his big competitors. He kept promoting the message that Wall Street research didn't really help clients avoid major losses in the stock market crash. Investors still licking their wounds only had to look at their brokerage statement to see Schwab was right.

One sign that Schwab was on the right track was the fact that the traditional brokerage firms absolutely hated Schwab. They felt threatened by his actions but were simply not equipped to do business in this no frills, discount way.

Instead, the big firms resorted to name calling and intimidation. They ran ads trying to scare investors away from Schwab. He retaliated by putting his name and photo in advertisements, inviting prospective clients to call him personally if they had concerns about the bad publicity.

At a time when all the major brokerage firms were nameless, faceless institutions, Charles Schwab opted to market himself – a real live human being. No other Wall Street firm did that. This was yet another way he tried to be unique and different from his competitors (another instance of Schwab following Rule #3 about using uniqueness to marginalize competitors).

Today, Schwab generates $5 billion a year in revenues and has a stock market value of approximately $18 billion. It's quite a remarkable journey from Schwab being a very small business in a sea of industry giants. But by following a few simple rules in its formative years, Charles Schwab & Co., Inc., became a recession-proof business.

The Common Thread

In the many examples of companies that truly thrived in a recession, you can see how each followed the recession-proof business formula. Their founders looked for opportunities when others were hunkering down (Rule #1). They focused on solving customer problems that got worse in a recession (Rule #2). Then, they solved these problems in a radically different and unique way, making them resistant to competition (Rule #3). Finally, once they had followed the first three rules, they aggressively marketed what they had to offer (Rule #4).

While each of the success story companies featured in this chapter and in previous ones followed these four rules, you'll notice how *differently* they did it. And that's the big point I want to make. Each of these companies had a unique approach to recession-proofing their business.

Companies like Charles Schwab and Hewlett-Packard developed and introduced innovative ways to solve customer problems that cost much less – and passed the savings along to customers. Disney beat competitors with films that were much richer and engaging than its competition's – winning because of the breathtaking quality of its films. Domino's Pizza competed on speed when others were competing on quality of food. Price Club competed on the combination of absurdly low unit prices and forcing customers to buy in quantities far greater than they ever normally would – radically changing the "what you get" and "what you pay" equation for buyers.

UPS competed on reliability in a sea of shady delivery services. Federal Express competed on speed of delivery and cost savings – when compared to clients chartering an entire plane (as opposed to the fact that Federal Express rates were 20 times higher than the US Postal Service). Coors competed through its geographical focus. And *Fortune* magazine competed by covering the business issues of the day in far greater depth than any other publication – and benefited when most Americans had just lost their life's savings in the Great Depression and were hungry for information on how to get their fortunes back.

Each company was different. There is no single right answer. You don't always have to compete on price. It's not always appropriate to compete on speed. At other times competing on reliability is the right move. But in each of these cases, the entrepreneurs behind these recession success story companies chose to do something radically different than the competition. And they did so in a way to harness the sporadic pockets of growing demand that were often only noticed by those actively looking for them.

Each company's unique situation required a unique approach to the four rules of recession-proofing your business. It's an important lesson to keep in mind.

From Concept to Execution

As we wrap up this section of the book, we shift from the big conceptual ideas behind creating a recession-proof business to the nuts and bolts of taking specific actions. Ideas are great, but they aren't worth much if they aren't executed in your business.

The next section is devoted to the critical topic of marketing in a recession. Marketing is the "tip of the spear" in your business. Marketing is the part of your business that potential buyers encounter first – before they meet your staff, try your products, or experience your service.

Unless you get your marketing right, nothing else matters. On that note, let's get started on the topic of specifically how to market your business in a recession.

Part II:
Recession Marketing

CHAPTER 6

How to Channel Customer Demand

The key to channeling market demand to drive sales of your products and services is to master the skill of marketing and, in particular, a specific form of marketing called direct response marketing.

Ninety percent of the marketing and advertising you see constitutes "image advertising" – not direct response advertising. Typically, these newspaper ads, Internet websites, Yellow Pages ads, direct mail pieces, and other image ads simply look like glorified business cards.

There are numerous problems with this kind of image advertising, including 1) it's not compelling to your prospective customer; 2) it doesn't work very well, especially if your marketing budget is less than $10 million a year; and 3) you can't track whether the image ad worked or not, so you can't improve it to make more money.

If you've had some success in your business, it is likely that you already have some idea of how to sell your products or services when you meet prospects face to face. Your prospects will have all kinds of questions with regard to how you can help them, what you charge, and why they should choose you over a competitor. Instinctively, you've become good at answering these basic questions in face-to-face selling situations.

Marketing is really just salesmanship multiplied across multiple media. You simply take your already successful sales message (that you deliver in person) and put it on your website, in direct mail, in newspaper ads, etc. While this is a bit of an oversimplification, it's not too much of one.

Image advertising is designed to build awareness and get your name out there. What it doesn't do is persuasively convince prospects to do business with you. Image ads do not sell. That's why they don't work.

As business owners, we don't pay our bills with awareness, we pay them with cash. And to generate cash, we must become good at selling our products and services in person, on the phone, and in our ads.

You might be wondering why so many companies use image advertising if it doesn't work. Unfortunately, I don't know the answer to this complex question either. Personally, I think Madison Avenue, where most of the world's largest advertising firms reside, is a confused place. If you're an advertising person on Madison Avenue, the most prestigious accomplishment you can achieve as an "ad man" is to win a Clio Award. Every year, Clio Awards are won by teams that make the most creative TV ads.

I find that criteria ridiculous. The only advertising person winning awards should be the person creating ads that make the most money, period.

Also, the incentives in the advertising industry are absolutely nuts. Most advertising agencies charge a 15 percent commission based on what they spend in advertising on your behalf.

Think about that for a moment.

If you have a teenager, would you give him your credit card and tell him that his allowance this week will be 15 percent of whatever he buys for you on your credit card?

What's the incentive? The incentive is to spend as much of your money as possible. The more of your money advertisers waste, the more money they make. That's just wrong.

Three features of direct response marketing that make it an ideal marketing method:

1. Direct response marketing "sells" and asks prospects to take action to do business with you (without any guesswork on their part or silent hope on your part that your prospects will figure out for themselves why they should do business with you).

2. All direct response marketing makes an "offer" to the prospect (either to buy, to call for more information, to make an appointment, or to visit your place of business).

3. Because all direct response marketing includes an offer, you can track its effectiveness (and continue doing the marketing that works, and stop doing the marketing that doesn't work).

It's this financial accountability characteristic that makes direct response marketing an attractive marketing tool in a recession. Because direct response ads can be tracked (unlike image advertising), it turns marketing from an expense to an investment. Done right, direct response marketing is financially quite predictable. You invest $X to make $Y. While it takes a little while to figure out what X and Y are, once you figure it out, repeating the process is straightforward.

Think of it this way. If all of your advertising consists of image advertising, you can't tell if it works or not. Therefore, marketing is treated as an expense because it actually is just an expense. If you're a smart business owner, you want to minimize expenses, and your inclination is to reduce the amount of money you waste on (image) advertising.

But, if you are able to track the financial return on investment for every single direct response ad you run, your advertising money is suddenly accountable and becomes an investment. For example, by tracking your results, you will know for a fact that a postcard, website, or advertisement you created generated five dollars in sales for every one dollar you invested in it. It doesn't take a genius to realize that if you can invest one dollar and make five dollars, you ought to do more of it.

That's what direct response marketing enables you to do. It allows you to clearly see where your money is going and what it's making for you.

Let me put it another way.

When you spend money on image advertising, it's like having a sales force that's paid on a straight salary and nobody is tracking what each person sells. You have no idea who is selling the most or who is selling the least. You have no idea which salesperson you should be sending your best prospects to and which salesperson you should probably get rid of. That's the world of image advertising.

When you use direct response marketing, every advertising piece – every ad, every direct mail piece, every web page, every email, every fax, every phone call – is accountable. Every marketing piece is like having a salesperson paid on commission. You know precisely who's making you money and who's not.

Most business owners intuitively understand this when it comes to managing salespeople, but unfortunately they do not apply this same "common sense" to their marketing. Instead, they underinvest in marketing because until now they've been flying blind when it comes to knowing how their marketing is performing.

In the next chapter, I'll reveal the magic words, or marketing message, you need to deliver to prospects to win them over as new customers. Getting the marketing message right is particularly important in a recession.

CHAPTER 7

How to Win Over Customers

After you find a way to communicate with prospects in a financially accountable way, the next step is to figure out what you're going to say to those prospects to turn them into customers.

Here's the challenge.

People are busy. There are a lot of competitors out there – all saying pretty much the same thing. "We're #1." "The Best Prices in Town." All this noise distracts people from paying attention to you and your marketing message. There's spam, billboards, cellphones, regular phones, email, faxes, junk mail, radio, TV ... you get the idea.

What you communicate to your prospects must cut instantly through all the clutter and explain clearly in just a few seconds why they should do business with you instead of with a competitor.

In a recession, the problem gets even worse as all the major forms of media are flooded with negative news about the economy. This not only adds to the marketplace noise but it causes fear and hesitation in the minds of many buyers.

That is why the ability to create a powerful message that gets noticed is an incredibly powerful competitive advantage. The strategy I'm about to reveal to you has been a key weapon in my marketing tool bag for years. It's simple, powerful, and easy.

The secret to making a prospect completely ignore your competitors and do business with you instead is to make the prospect a "Unique, Compelling, and Credible Promise (UCCP)."

I'll elaborate on this powerful UCCP formula in a moment and explain how using this formula can allow you to dominate a market. But first, let me show you why the key to dominating a market is being able to go head-to-head against a competitor for just one prospective customer – and win nearly every time.

Imagine that you and all your top competitors are competing for just one customer. Let's call her Mary.

Here's what Mary is going to do.

She's going to call your office, visit your place of business, or browse your website (or however you typically do business). She is going to make contact with your business, spend three minutes learning about what you have to offer, and then repeat that process with all your competitors.

Your job is to make sure Mary picks your company as the overwhelmingly obvious choice that she should select.

I call this the "Mary Test."

Forget about marketing, market share, competition, and all that stuff. The goal of your marketing is to win Mary over 9 times out of 10. It's that simple.

If you've figured out a way to win Mary over 9 times out of 10, it's actually very easy to multiply your success across more and more prospects.

If you can win Mary's business, you can certainly win John's, Clara's, and Bob's business too. But if you can't win Mary's business, you're going to be destroyed in the marketplace.

The key to this secret is to focus on winning over just one prospect when you're competing head-to-head with your top competitors.

How do you do this?

Here's the formula. You want to communicate the following to Mary:

- Unique
- Compelling
- Credible
- Promise

Communicate a promise of what she'll get by doing business with you. That promise needs to be unique (and different from that of your competitors); it must be compelling (and provide a huge benefit that she actually wants); and it must be credible (meaning you must be able to prove you can deliver on that promise).

Let me walk you through each one of these.

First, to win Mary over, you need to make Mary a promise. That's the first step. Most companies never make their prospects a promise – so they don't get many prospects to become customers.

The second step is to make the promise a unique promise.

Here's a simple exercise. Pick up the local Yellow Pages and flip to any section with a lot of listings. Look at the ads. You'll notice something – they all look alike. First, most of the ads are image ads that are nothing more than a glorified business card. Second, (and more important), those ads all say the same thing. "We're #1," "We're the best," "We treat you right," etc.

It's impossible to win Mary over if what you promise is the same as what all your competitors are saying. Mary has a lot of options to choose from and when you and your competitors all look the same, there is no reason in particular for Mary to choose you over a competitor.

How to Make Your Promise Unique

Here's how to make a promise unique. Every promise consists of five components that make it either unique or similar to other promises.

Here are the five components of every promise:

- **Whom** you're making the promise to
- **What** you're promising them
- **Where** you plan to deliver that promise
- **When** you'll deliver your promise
- **How** you'll deliver your promise

To make your promise unique, simply change one of the five components of your promise.

Change Who You Are Targeting With Your Promise

Let's start with *who*.

This is an easy one – simply specialize in whom you serve. If you're an insurance broker selling to anyone and everyone, you can specialize in serving small businesses. You can tell your prospects that you specialize by exclusively serving small businesses. If you're competing in a field of insurance agents who are all serving small-business owners, you can specialize even further and focus just on restaurants, retail stores, or any one of a number of niche industries. The more specialized your target audience, the more compelling your promise automatically becomes.

If you own a pizza restaurant, rather than compete with the millions of pizza places out there, you can shift *whom* you serve to another audience, such as kids. Your pizza place only specializes in serving kids who want to have fun. Chuck E. Cheese did this amazingly well and after decades of searching, I have yet to find another pizza place trying to compete with them for the kids audience.

If you're a doctor, you can specialize in serving a particular demographic group like Spanish speakers. The Hispanic market is one of the fastest growing demographic markets in the United States right now. Many large companies have formed entire divisions just to serve this market. If you have the skills to do so, there's no reason you can't too.

Babies "R" Us specializes in selling toys, supplies, and other things needed for babies – and only babies.

USAA is an insurance company that specializes in providing insurance to members of the military and their families.

The AARP – American Association of Retired People – originally started out as an insurance company that exclusively served seniors. It did such a good job catering to that audience that most people mistakenly thought it was an association long before it made the actual transition.

The list goes on and on. The advantage of picking a very specific "who" is that in less than 15 seconds your prospects can instantly understand and appreciate the advantages they will receive by doing business with you – even if everything else you have to offer is the same as your competitors. Just the fact that you specialize in serving a very specific audience has a very powerful effect in attracting prospects of that type to you.

Change What You Are Promising

Another way to differentiate yourself from your competition is to change what you promise to deliver. In the auto industry, a few smart auto dealers are bundling prepaid maintenance with all the cars they sell. Rather than sell a car and let their customers price shop on the Internet and with all the other dealers across town, they sell "Zero Hassles, Zero Repair Bills, Zero Car Wash

Bills, Zero Oil Change Bills for two years." While every other dealer in town is selling cars, they're selling "no hassle transportation" at a fixed price with no surprise repair bills. All oil changes, routine maintenance, and car washes for two years are already included. That's a great example of changing *what* you promise to your customers.

Sometimes you can promise your customers *less* and turn that into a benefit. One of the fastest growing grocery store chains is Whole Foods. It specializes primarily in stocking organic fruits and vegetables. Its promise is that it provides you and your family with fresh produce *without* the pesticides that are normally used by farmers who supply competitive grocery stores.

As traditional grocery stores started expanding their organic food sections to compete with Whole Foods, Whole Foods responded by morphing its own promise to keep itself unique. Instead of just promising organic foods, it now promises "locally grown" foods. My guess is its competitors truck their produce halfway across the country, whereas Whole Foods doesn't. Because of this structural difference that makes it hard for competitors to change, Whole Foods is going after the "locally grown" promise. But that promise is unique, and only time will tell if customers find the new promise compelling as well.

One benefit of making *what* you promise different from your competitors' is that you can charge more money for what you have to offer. Actually, this is true whenever you make your promise unique (whether you differentiate via the Who, What, Where, When, or How).

For example, our family shops almost exclusively at Whole Foods. But when my wife and I did the math, we realized we were spending nearly double the amount we would have if we had just walked across the street to shop at a conventional grocery store. We do so because we happen to value *what* they promise –apparently a lot more than just money! Many of our friends (who also have young kids and don't want them to eat pesticides) also shop there. We even have a nickname for Whole Foods. We call it "Whole Paycheck" because of how much more things cost. Yet we still love it, still shop there, and still recommend it to others. That's the power of making a promise unique – just make sure what you promise is very different from what your competitors do.

Here's another example. Dell Computers sells all of its computers through direct mail, via the Internet, and by telephone. I've noticed more recently that to compete more effectively with local stores that offer to set up the computer for you in your home, Dell also offers "in-home installation" when you buy your PC online. Instead of just selling PC computers in a box, it now sells working computers that you don't have to unpack or set up – it's all done for you.

I have one client who's a mortgage broker competing against hundreds, if not thousands, of mortgage brokers in his area. A few weeks ago, he asked me how he should sell an innovative new loan product that was not yet widely available among competing lenders. He was having difficulty explaining the value of this program to his prospects and was looking for help. I didn't understand all the financial and technical jargon and I suspect most of his prospects didn't either. When discussing this product, he was using a lot of technical language. This resulted in his prospects being confused and unclear about what he was promising and how it was different than the competition.

After a lot of digging, we realized that the primary benefit of this program was that it would allow most people to own their home outright, typically five to seven years faster than with other loan products – without any fluctuation in their monthly payment. I suggested that he talk about the program as a "fast track to retirement" program. Instead of promising X percent interest rate for Y years, he should paint the program as a way to get on the "fast track to early retirement." After the prospects expressed interest, he could explain all the technical mumbo jumbo. The mortgage industry is very regulated, so at last check he was looking into any restrictions there might be on how he communicates his promise to his clients.

The lesson in all this is that changing what you promise can instantly make your promise to customers unique.

Change Where You'll Deliver What You Promise

Another way to make your promise unique is to change *where* the customer gets to enjoy the benefits you promise.

Here are several examples:

In the dry cleaning business, everybody seems to compete on price. One dry cleaner I know of deliberately charges more, a lot more, per item than any of his competitors. He is successful with the higher prices because, unlike his competitors, his company will pick up at and deliver your dry cleaning directly to your front door. For a lot of people, the hassle of going to the dry cleaner to drop off and pick up clothes is a big pain. For these very busy people, they now have the option of completely eliminating that hassle from their lives.

Subway is one of the fastest growing fast food franchises in the world. In its first seven years or so of existence, it exceeded the number of locations that took its competitor, McDonald's, more than 50 years to establish. It did this in part by promising its customers access to fast food in locations in which McDonald's was not legally allowed to operate. As I understand it, McDonald's and other similar fast food restaurants that have grills require extensive ventilation exhaust systems to keep the air clean. Because of this health code requirement, only certain kinds of properties (usually stand-alone) could meet these requirements.

Subway, on the other hand, does not do any grilling. Most of its food is either served cold, heated in a microwave, or baked. As a result, Subway could open locations in tiny strip malls, inside gas stations, in shopping malls – all places where McDonald's was *not* located. By changing *where* it would deliver on its promise, it was able to establish more restaurant locations than even McDonald's.

Here's a simple method for experimenting with where you'll deliver on the promise you make to prospects. If your prospects normally come to you to do business, consider finding a way to take your product and service directly to them instead (and charge more than your competitors). You can also try the reverse. If you and your competitors normally go to your prospects, try having them come to you instead (and perhaps pass on the cost savings to your customers).

Change When You'll Deliver on Your Promise

In today's fast-paced world, you can often experiment with changing the speed at which you'll deliver on your promise. Federal Express made its mark by promising to get your packages there "absolutely, positively" the next day. Domino's made similar promises with its pizza delivered to your door in "30 minutes or less, guaranteed."

Norwalk Furniture offers custom built furniture exactly to your specifications in a fraction of the time it usually takes for other companies to do the same.

You can often charge more for faster service because a lot of people want things now, now, now.

Ironically, you can also make your promise unique by offering to deliver your product slower than your competition. Baja Fresh is a fast food chain that serves Mexican food. Rather than prepare all of your food in advance, it only cooks it after you order it. Its promise differs from other fast food companies in two ways. First, it makes the claim that the food is better (changing what it promises). Second, it promises to take longer to cook your food than its competitors. Its argument is that it deliberately takes longer to cook your food so that it will taste better. Interestingly, it makes the "you get your food slower" promise a benefit.

You can also change your hours of operation. Kinko's came to dominate the local print shop industry by staying open 24 hours a day, 7 days a week, 365 days a year. When I was a Stanford University student, I would sometimes finish a term paper or a résumé at 3 a.m. and desperately need to get it printed. I would drive down to the Kinko's on California Avenue in Palo Alto and pay whatever it cost. I didn't even look at the prices and I still don't! I go to Kinko's when I absolutely need something right now regardless of what time of day or night it is.

Interestingly, I've been tracking Kinko's prices over the years. Originally, its prices were fairly similar to that of its competitors. As its 9-to-5 competitors fell by the wayside, I've noticed that the prices have crept up over the years and seem a little higher than others. Personally, I don't care because when I want something printed urgently it is the only place I know that can deliver.

Now that Federal Express has acquired Kinko's, it has combined this 24x7 "when" promise with a twist in its "where" promise. Now you don't even have to go into your local Kinko's store. You can submit your entire print job directly over the Internet and have the option of picking it up in a few hours. Or, Federal Express will deliver it to your front door "absolutely, positively" the next day, so you don't even have to leave your house.

I hope by now you're seeing how very successful companies have made billions, if not tens of billions, of dollars by simply making a small change in the promises they make to customers.

Change How You Deliver on Your Promise

The final way you can make your promise unique is to change *how* you deliver on your promises. Here are several examples of this.

Starbucks serves premium coffee exactly the way you want and with a friendly smile. You can have your coffee decaf, caffeinated, or extra caffeinated. You can have skim milk, 1 percent fat milk, whole milk, or soy milk. You can have Tall, Grande (medium), or Venti (large). It can be hot or cold. You can add flavored syrup to your coffee. If you decide to add syrup, you have multiple choices. You can add foam to the top. You can have your coffee in any one of several hundred combinations.

Rather than just serving you any cup of coffee, Starbucks creates a cup of coffee just for you, exactly the way you want it.

Benihana is a Japanese restaurant that competes against a lot of other Japanese restaurants. The difference at Benihana is that your food is cooked right in front of you. The chefs are trained to put on a show by tossing the food and using their cooking supplies right in front of you. This has the very deliberate consequence of dramatically changing what they deliver to you. When you go to Benihana, you're not going there for dinner. You're going there for dinner and a show. That's the power of changing the *how* part of your promise to customers.

The Starbucks of the ice cream business is Cold Stone Creamery. It takes ordinary ice cream and mixes in one, two, or more mix-ins such as cookies, crumbled candy bars, fruit, nuts, and more. It is all mixed up right in front of you, on a frozen stone, and served to you with a smile; sometimes they even sing a song if you give them a tip. This isn't about ice cream at all; it's about enjoying an entertaining experience.

Countless numbers of small and large companies alike have built their businesses by making a truly unique promise to prospects and customers. By simply changing one or two elements of the typical promise made in your industry, you can have a dramatic effect on stimulating overwhelming market demand for your product. The keys are to alter the Who, What, Where, When, or How components of your promise.

By doing this you can win Mary over from your competitors. Keep in mind – the secret to dominating your market starts with the "Mary Test" first. You must find a way to win Mary over despite head-to-head competition from your competitors. As you'll discover soon enough, if you can win customers over in one-on-one situations, you can easily multiply that to win customers by the hundreds and thousands.

Let me start by showing you how to make your promise more compelling.

How to Make Your Promise Compelling

A compelling promise is one that provides a big benefit to your customers – one that the customer actually wants. It really doesn't matter what your prospects or customers need; what matters is what they want, desire, or must have. Many businesses have failed by providing what customers needed but what nobody really ever wanted.

The first key to making your promise compelling is to solve a problem that your prospect already knows he has and already wants solved.

The second is to provide not just a little benefit but a dramatic and big benefit to your customer. The combination of the two is incredibly powerful.

Let's revisit the promise that Domino's Pizza used:

"Fresh, Hot Pizza Delivered to Your Door
in 30 Minutes or Less ... Guaranteed!"

Domino's Pizza used that promise to build a multi-billion-dollar company from one single restaurant located in a college town. It solves a really pressing problem – "I'm Starving" – and it provides a big benefit – its promise of "30 minutes or less, guaranteed!" Now that's a compelling promise.

The company no longer uses that promise due to some liability issues with their drivers speeding to get food to customers fast. But, despite this fact, Domino's Pizza exists, in large part, because of its compelling promise.

Here's another compelling promise from Costco. While Costco doesn't explicitly make this promise, we loyal Costco shoppers figured it out on our own. "Rock bottom wholesale prices on name-brand merchandise if you're willing to buy in bulk." Costco is perfect for anyone who uses a lot of "everyday stuff" and wants high quality with low prices. I buy all my paper towels, toilet paper, and bottled water there. I love the place because it offers me a compelling promise, and I know exactly what I'm going to get when I go there. It's a crystal clear, compelling promise.

Here's an example of a promise that a company got wrong. It promised to solve a problem that its customers did not want solved. This consumer goods company was developing a universal cleanser. This one cleanser could be used to wash your clothes, clean your toilet, wash your car, or clean your carpets. Just one tub of this stuff could clean everything in your house, even you. The problem is customers didn't want to use the same cleaner to clean themselves and their toilet bowl. Go figure!

The product did not sell well. As I understand, the company later created five versions of the product, each with a specific and unique promise. It created a bathroom cleaner to clean bathrooms, a carpet cleaner to clean carpets, and a laundry detergent to wash your laundry. Each version of this product had a unique, compelling, and credible promise that the product did indeed deliver on – even though all essentially had the same ingredients as the original product. The reinvented versions sold a lot better than the universal cleaner.

Here are two key tips to make your promise compelling:

Solve a problem that your customer already knows he or she has, wants to get solved, and is willing to pay to get rid of.

Solve that problem in a powerful way and provide dramatic value in your promise.

How to Make Your Promise Credible

Using this approach, you've communicated a promise to your prospect. You've made sure the promise is unique and compelling. Now you want to make your promise as credible as possible. This means you need to provide easy-to-believe *proof* that you can deliver on your promise.

There are several ways to provide proof. Here are a number of them:

- *Show testimonials.* Show Mary dozens, if not hundreds, of testimonial letters.

- *Be specific.* If you have the best selection in town and in stock, prove it. Tell Mary exactly how many items are in stock: 45,237 items in stock all the time is much more credible than "best selection in town."

- *Give a compelling reason why.* If you have the lowest prices in town, you'd better be able to explain *why* you have the lowest prices in town. Everybody else uses a middleman – you cut out the middleman and pass the savings on. Or you're located in an out-of-the way location that has much lower rent, and you pass the savings on – all she has to do is drive an extra 10 minutes.

- *Offer a guarantee.* Offer a money-back guarantee. If you fail to live up to your promises, offer to refund her money. This is a powerful "put your money where your mouth is" type of promise. If your competitors make the same promises as you, but you know they can't deliver, guarantee your results and you'll win.

(If you're really, really gutsy, offer a double- your-money-back guarantee. I tried this once on a particular product and I doubled my net profits. My refunds did go up a little, but my sales more than doubled and compensated for the refunds with a bunch of extra profit to boot.)

Obviously, you really had better be able to deliver on your promises or you shouldn't do this – but it's a very simple way to separate yourself from the competition.

To recap, to win over a single prospect, Mary, in direct head-to-head competition, make a Unique, Compelling, and Credible Promise.

It's vitally important to focus on winning over just one customer at a time, because that's how the battle for market dominance is won.

The key to winning new customers is to make them a Unique, Compelling, and Credible Promise that answers the question, "Why should I do business with you instead of with your competitors?"

When you have a good answer to that question, you're ready to roll out your promise to more and more people.

CHAPTER 8

Make Marketing an Investment, Not an Expense

In the previous chapter, we discussed the importance of being able to win over customers one at a time. In this chapter, we'll talk about how to get your unique, compelling, and credible promise in front of prospective customers.

One word of caution: There is really no point in spending any money on marketing, advertising, or sales until you have a unique, compelling, and credible promise to make prospects.

I work with a lot of business owners, all of whom either spend way too much or way too little on marketing. If you aren't making a unique, compelling, and credible promise to the marketplace, spending even one dollar on marketing is way too much. There really is no point at all, as you're just another one of many options available to customers.

On the flip side, if you're making an incredibly unique, compelling, and credible promise to the market, then you've most likely underinvested in marketing.

This chapter will show you how to invest your money in marketing, instead of just spending your money on marketing. The difference between the two is accountability.

Accountable marketing means every marketing investment you make has a measurable and factual return on investment. Every other form of marketing is just guesswork and is an expense.

The logic of marketing that's accountable is extraordinarily compelling.

Let me ask you: If you spent $100 on a newspaper advertisement and you made $500 from the sales generated by that advertisement, would you run the advertisement again? Of course you would. Anytime you can make a 500 percent return on investment from marketing (or anything), you repeat it.

Now let me ask you a slightly different question.

If you spent $100 on a newspaper advertisement and you have no idea whether you made any money from the advertisement, would you repeat the expense? Well, this is a tough question, because maybe you're making money from that advertisement and maybe you're not. It's hard to say. The only correct answer is "I'm not sure."

Now let's increase the stakes.

Let's say you've invested $100,000 in several marketing campaigns over the course of a year. If you're using marketing that's accountable, you'll know exactly how much profit you've made from your investment in those campaigns. If you know that you've made $500,000 directly from those campaigns, would you keep the campaign going? Of course you would. The answer is as clear as night and day.

Now assume you're spending $100,000 on a marketing campaign that isn't accountable. You have no idea how much money you've made from it. Would you keep doing it? Again, the answer is not clear, but the penalty for making the wrong decision is steep.

Accountable Marketing Is a Hidden Advantage

When your marketing is accountable, it provides you with an enormous advantage in the marketplace. You have great clarity on what marketing activities are making you money and what activities are not.

When you're investing $100 to make $300, $500, or even $1,000 using a particular marketing campaign, it's a lot easier to justify increasing your investment 10-fold. Instead of investing $100 to make $500, you can now invest $1,000 to make $5,000. If investing $1,000 to make $5,000 works, you can invest $10,000 to make $50,000 and so on.

Let me share a personal example of how I had great success using this exact strategy.

How I Grew Sales of One Product Line from $500 per Month to $30,000 per Month in 90 Days

A few years ago, I was starting a new product line and my sales went from $500 a month to $30,000 a month in 90 days. Keep in mind that this was a product with no track record, no previous buyers, and no established reseller channel. It was a product line started literally from scratch. The speed of that growth surprised even me, but the process was actually quite simple.

When I first started that project, I was not sure what advertising options would work nor was I sure what unique, compelling, credible promise would work best. I started by running three very small advertisements – each with a different promise in it. Each ad probably cost me $100. Out of the three ads, one ad made me $150 while the other two ads each made me $25.

Out of the total investment, I spent $300 on marketing but only generated $200 in sales, so I lost $100 on the investment.

How did I turn a $100 loss into $30,000 in sales 88 days later?

I started first by modifying the one ad that worked the best – the ad that cost me $100 but generated $150 in revenue. I took the promise in that ad and experimented with changing it to make it unique, more compelling, and more credible. Based on the sales results, my prospects were "voting" on which promise they liked more. So I simply gave them more ads to vote on.

I really like the concept that money is really just a way for customers to vote on what they like. If something makes you money, it means customers like what you offer and are voting for you to continue doing it.

I ran another cycle of test ads. I took my best ad from the first cycle, the one where I spent $100 and made $150, then created a few additional variations. The best ad from the second cycle cost me $100 and I made $175.

During that 90-day period, I ran between 20 and 30 advertising cycles and ultimately found a winning promise that allowed me to make $200 in sales for every $100 I spent on marketing (this was for a very high-margin product). Once I had the winning promise right, I simply bought more ad space. Instead of investing just $300 a week in advertising, I slowly increased the investment to $1,000 a week. When my return on investment held at the new investment level, I went to $2,000 a week. Then I went to $3,000 a week and finally capped out at $3,500 a week in marketing investments. After 90 days I was investing about $15,000 a month in marketing to generate $30,000 a month in sales for a very high-margin product.

Here's the key lesson from accountable marketing and why I think it's flat-out crazy to do marketing any other way.

Accountable marketing allows you to start on a very small marketing budget yet scale up quickly when it works. In a recession, it's a smart way to manage risk carefully – limiting downside losses while preserving upside potential.

It allows you to get feedback and "votes" from the marketplace on what promises prospects like the most. Once you find a winning promise, it's very easy to buy more ads, buy bigger ads, or run your ads more often. Increasing the exposure of your ad is much easier than creating an ad with a winning promise inside it.

That's why I will continually emphasize and remind you that you must work on winning over customers one at a time. The key is to make them a unique, compelling, and credible promise.

If you can't win over one customer at a time, how in the world will you win over 100 customers at a time or 1,000 customers at a time? You won't.

Keep it simple. Create your winning promise and win over customers one at a time. Once you've been able to accomplish that and *only* after you've accomplished that does it make sense to get your promise out there to more prospects.

What Is Accountable Marketing?

Accountable marketing is simply any form of marketing that asks the prospect to take an action that is measurable on your end. Here are several examples:

- An advertisement that invites the reader to call your office and ask for extension 101.

- A direct mail piece that asks the prospect to visit your store and bring in this 10 percent off coupon (the coupon has Coupon #102 printed on it).

- A fax broadcast to previous customers that asks them to fax your office to request "Free Consumer Guide – Report #103."

- An email message to existing customers telling them to visit your website to pick up an electronic version of your free consumer guide at www.yoursite.com/report104.

You'll notice that what all these accountable marketing examples have in common is some type of tracking mechanism – extension 101, coupon 102, etc. When each order is taken from customers, make note of which marketing investment generated the sale. If you made $500 from marketing investment #101, keep track of it. If marketing investment #102 (the coupon) generates $1,000, keep track of that too.

Once a week or once a month (depending on your business), tally the scores and see how each investment did. If investment #101 made you $400, keep doing it next month. If investment #102 lost you money, either try a different version of the promise or stop it entirely. Simply keep repeating the process by trimming your losers and expanding your winners.

The other less obvious benefit to using this kind of marketing is that it can grow your revenues very quickly without adding a lot of overhead, infrastructure, or staff.

Here's an actual example of marketing that's accountable. When I want to generate leads for my products and consulting services, I will run ads that look similar to this:

Free Special Report:
How to Take Your Business to the Next Level

To request this free report, call 800-333-3011, ext. 103, for a free, 24-hour recorded message for details. Call any time, day or night.

By the way, that's a real working phone number that you're welcome to call anytime. When you call, you'll hear a recording of my voice (you didn't think I'd answer that phone live, did you?) asking prospects to leave a mailing address where I can send them the free report. The free report then provides additional information on my products and services.

This is an example of an advertisement that's accountable. When the prospect calls that particular extension, I know exactly which ad in which publication generated that prospect. That's because every time I run the ad, I use a different extension so I can track the return on investment of my advertisements.

As a reader of this book, you're encouraged to call my information request line 800-333-3011, ext. 103, to see how I set this up. When you call this toll-free number, you'll not only hear my regular outgoing message, you'll also hear a "behind the scenes" explanation of how I'm using this marketing tool and making it accountable.

I like marketing that's accountable for several reasons. First, it eliminates a lot of risk from my marketing investments. Like the 800 number example above, it's also lifestyle friendly. I can simply set up my marketing systems to ensure that they are accountable and will work for me 24 hours a day, 7 days a week while I spend time with my family.

Second, accountable marketing can enable you to grow a business very quickly without a lot of overhead. In my earlier example of growing one segment of my business from $500 to $30,000 in 90 days, I didn't have to hire any sales reps, I didn't have to lease a bigger office, I didn't have to buy any delivery trucks, and I didn't need a bigger warehouse. All I needed to do was increase my monthly advertising investment, which only took a few minutes, and add more capacity to my customer service operations.

In short, using marketing that's accountable has been an effective strategy for me, and I would encourage you to use it. It's well suited for businesses of any size – but is certainly mandatory for any business on a limited budget. At the same time, it allows you to grow your business very quickly once you find a winning promise to make to customers.

CHAPTER 9

Marketing Is All About Timing

One of my marketing mentors, Dan Kennedy, says that marketing is all about timing. The difference between yesterday's dinner salad and today's trash is timing. I couldn't agree more.

When I critique marketing pieces from clients, I often notice a huge timing mistake that wastes a lot of money. I call this the "Don't Propose Marriage Before Asking for the First Date" timing problem.

Don't Skip the First Date!

One of the most common mistakes I see in advertising and marketing is that of companies routinely selling the wrong "thing" in their ads. Rather than selling the next step in the sales process, such as "call my office" or "visit our store," they try to sell their product or service right in the advertisement itself. That's a big timing mistake.

It's the equivalent of asking someone to marry you before asking for the first date – a serious timing error. Why is proposing marriage before the first date a major timing mistake? First, just because you want to jump to the end of the dating process doesn't mean the other person also wants to do so. Second, it doesn't match the other person's decision-making process. When you violate the other person's decision-making process, you actually end up repelling (not attracting) him or her. In short, it's too big a leap in commitment too quickly.

The same is true with most advertising. Most advertising is created assuming the buyer is going to make an immediate purchase decision on the spot – before requesting more information, before calling to make an appointment, before visiting your place of business. Yet for most businesses, the business owner doesn't actually expect a person to buy the advertised product or service without requesting additional information, but that's the way the ads are written.

Here's an example. A client of mine, a mortgage broker, wrote a letter (an advertisement) to his past clients to promote a new loan product. The letter included a lot of technical language that he is legally required to disclose before originating a new loan.

This was a timing mistake. So I asked him, "How many times have you sent a letter like this and the person writes you back and says, 'Okay, sign me up'?" His reply was, "That never happens. I always end up with a phone appointment or an in-person appointment to exchange a lot of information before the prospects can make a decision and before I'm legally allowed to let them make a decision."

In response to this information, here's what I said: "Your letter is asking them to accept the loan before they've had a chance to talk with you. You're proposing marriage before asking for the first date. In a nutshell, in your letter, stop selling the loan; sell the meeting instead."

My advice to him was that instead of promoting the loan in the advertisement, he should instead "sell the meeting." Rather than provide a unique, compelling, and credible promise that his product can offer to the prospect, he should provide a unique, compelling, and credible promise on why the prospect should meet with him.

To translate into dating terms, you don't sell a woman on a first date by telling her how she'll love having you as a husband. You sell the first date by telling her how she'll have a great time on the first date. It's all just timing.

Here's another way you can see thousands of timing mistakes in advertising. Open your local newspaper or your Yellow Pages and you'll see a lot of timing mistakes. Most advertisers are proposing marriage without asking for the first date. You'll often see specific product and service descriptions. Sometimes you'll see prices listed. For almost all the products and services featured in these ads, the sales process typically requires visiting a store, making a telephone call, or scheduling an appointment. Rather than trying to sell a product that prospects can't buy on the spot, they are better off selling the prospect on the benefits of visiting the store, calling the advertiser, or scheduling an appointment. Once the prospect shows up at the store, calls the office, or schedules an in-person meeting, you will be able to sell the prospect on the product or service you offer.

Mapping Your Marketing to a
Step-by-Step Sales Process

To get the timing aspect of your marketing right, start by mapping out a sales process. This process describes the step-by-step actions you want your prospects to take that result in them spending money with you. I'll use a simple retail store example. The process could be:

1. Customer visits store

2. Salesperson asks customer questions and recommends product

3. Salesperson rings up sale and offers extended warranty cross-sell

That's a fairly typical sales process for a retail oriented business. If you're selling a service to another business, it might be something like this:

1. Client schedules appointment

2. Evaluate client situation and recommend solution

3. Write contract and collect payment

You'll notice in each of these sales processes, step #1 – visit store or schedule an appointment – is *not* a financial transaction. The financial transaction occurs in step #3. As result, your marketing should focus on selling the prospect on the value of step #1 and nothing other than the value of step #1.

You have to give some thought to the sales process in your business and match your marketing message to sell prospects on taking the first (not the final) step in your sales promise. Figure out the kind of "first date" you want with your prospect, and sell the first date – and whatever you do, don't propose marriage before you ask for the first date!

CHAPTER 10

The Chief Rainmaking Officer

In a previous chapter, I shared the story about how I grew one of my product lines from $500 a month to $30,000 a month in 90 days. Now, I'm going to share the story of how I took that $30,000-a-month product line and shrunk it to $15,000 in three days. As you'll recall, I grew that product line by systematically trying new promises in my ads and tracking the results. Because I was using direct response marketing that's accountable, I could drop the least profitable ads and keep experimenting with the most profitable ads.

As you might imagine, I was thrilled with the very fast revenue growth. This continued for about half a year until in a span of three days, my sales from that product line dropped by 50 percent. Here's what happened. At the time, my marketing for that product line consisted of running ads in only one advertising source. One hundred percent of my income from that product line was tied to a single source of leads and new customers. That publication made a simple policy change that required me to run my ads half as often as I used to. Within three days, my ads were showing half as often, resulting in a 50 percent drop in revenue almost overnight.

That one policy change cost me $180,000 in revenues over the next 12 months. While I was disappointed, I realized that I had made an enormous mistake. My entire marketing effort was tied to a single source of advertising, a single way to get prospects, a single customer source. I had all my marketing eggs in one basket.

I have a saying that in entrepreneurship there are no failures – only successes and lessons. Through that experience I learned a huge lesson – I needed to acquire new customers from multiple sources. The other thing I got was an $180,000 "tuition" bill courtesy of the school of hard knocks.

The rest of this chapter shows you how to insulate your income from volatility. It shows you both the mechanics of how to do this and the role you personally must take in making this happen.

The three keys to income stability are 1) recognizing your role as a Rainmaker; 2) continually finding new sources of customers (e.g., new places to advertise profitably, new market segments to target, new distribution channels to target); and 3) once you tap into a new source of customers, get your team to serve those customers while you stay focused on finding additional sources of new business.

Here's where most people go wrong. They start their business and stumble upon one, maybe two, customer sources that produce some results for them. Once they find something that works, they stick with it. There is nothing inherently wrong with this approach except that it's extremely complacent. Just because you have one customer source that works does not mean you should not look to establish additional ones.

One of the reasons some companies fail in a recession is an over-reliance on too few customer sources and revenue streams. In a booming economy, a rising tide lifts all boats. A strong economy can mask the fragility of a business that is over-reliant on too few customer sources. But when the economy turns or the company hits a bump in the road, all the weaknesses in the business suddenly become exposed.

The Chief Rainmaking Officer

As the CEO of your company, it's your role to be the Chief Rainmaking Officer. Rainmakers are the people most responsible for generating revenues for a business – they're the chief marketers for the business. If your business is profitable and growing like crazy, it's because you did a great job of being the Rainmaker. If your business isn't growing at all, that means you're not doing a good job as a Rainmaker or you aren't spending enough time on "rainmaking."

This point cannot be stated strongly enough. Your role must shift from "operating the business" to "growing the business." You absolutely must reduce the time you personally spend in operations and shift it to revenue generation – and in particular in establishing new revenues sources that are then managed by your team. You must become a Rainmaker.

The Rainmaker's #1 Job – Finding New Sources of Customers

As your business's Rainmaker, your #1 job today, tomorrow, and forever is to find new sources of customers to tap into.

Think of each new customer source as the equivalent of an oil well – something that has enormous profit potential. Your job as a Rainmaker is to spend your time drilling for new oil wells (customer sources) because it's the single most profitable, highly paid use of your time. Once you strike oil, bring in your team to pump out all the oil. This frees you to go drilling for new oil wells.

If you're very good at finding new oil wells (e.g., you really know how to market), you can pay others to pump out all the oil for you (e.g., fulfill on promises made to your customers).

If you don't do this, you'll spend all your time trying to pump out all the oil from just a single well. This is fine temporarily, but at some point that oil well will run dry and you'll be on the feast or famine roller-coaster ride that in a recession can be lethal.

I dedicate one day a week, Wednesday, to "drill for oil" or to look for and tap into new sources of customers. I keep my calendar clear on Wednesdays just to look for new customer sources that I can tap into. I don't take any phone calls; I don't do any client work; I just drill for oil on Wednesdays.

Whether you dedicate a whole day a week to new customer sources or an afternoon a week or an hour a day, some portion of your schedule must be focused on this critical activity.

How to Evolve into Your Rainmaker Role

If you're like many business owners I know, here's how your story goes. You launched your business by offering a promise to your prospects that was *not* especially unique, compelling, or credible. You simply promised the same thing as your competitors. In most cases, your prospects couldn't see how you were different from your competitors, so they did not reward you with their business.

Because of the lack of business, you can't afford to build a team and get others to do the operational work for you. Because you have to take care of customers personally, most of your week is spent on operations and you only take on the role of "Rainmaker" when you have no customers to serve.

You cycle back and forth between feast and famine. When you get a lot of customers, you get so busy taking care of them that you stop generating new business. For a while you feast off of the new customers then eventually you don't have enough business to sustain you. So you end up back in the famine mode desperately looking for new customers.

Here's specifically how you break this cycle:

It all starts with marketing, specifically with crafting and communicating a unique, compelling, credible promise. You keep working on your promise until it's truly unique, definitely compelling, and incredibly credible (with a lot of proof and testimonials to back up your promises). Once you have the promises in place, you want to charge above-average prices. Charging above-average prices only works if what you have to offer is unique, more compelling, or more credible than what your competitors have to offer. If you're not unique, more compelling, or more credible, you'll have a very hard time charging above-average prices. Again, crafting a unique, compelling, credible promise is the key to charging higher prices and breaking out of this cycle.

Once you have a winning promise in place, use that promise with your existing sources of new customers. Charge prices that are slightly higher than your competitors and use that extra money to hire the staff needed to manage your operations. The kind of help you need varies depending on the business you're in. What you do need to do is get someone else to handle the most time consuming, lowest revenue producing activities that you currently do personally. This can be an employee, a contractor, or a vendor. I tend to lump them all together as "team members."

Take the time you've just freed (initially it might only be one to three hours a week) and apply it toward rainmaking activities.

Use the time to create ads and test different places to advertise. Start small and increase your marketing investments on the profitable sources and shrink or eliminate your investments on the unprofitable sources.

When you get a source to work for you, congratulations! You just found another oil well. Now take the money you make from that lead source (the oil well) and pay to expand your team to handle the fulfillment of the promises you made to those customers. In other words, get your team to pump all the oil out of the well for you.

Use your time to continue to look for, test, and tap new customer sources. Repeat the process over and over. Once you've exhausted all the possible sources for new customers, work on establishing new revenue streams. These can be new products or new services or finding new markets to go after.

That's the Rainmaker's role in a nutshell. It's where you need to focus your time in order to prosper in a recession. So pay attention to where your time goes today, and work to shift an increasing amount of it toward rainmaking activities. It's a key step to recession-proofing your business.

CHAPTER 11

Unlock the Hidden Profits
in Your Business

One of the fastest ways to immediately improve the cash flow of a business is to unlock the hidden profits residing in the company's customer base. Here's why.

Acquiring new customers is one of the most important things your business must do to grow. But the challenge of acquiring new customers is that it's one of the most expensive activities. You invest a lot of money in marketing to acquire a customer just to get one sale. This initial sale is where your effective profit margins are the lowest. Not only do you have to use the revenues to cover the cost of your product or service, you have to use it to cover the cost of marketing. That doesn't leave much room for profit.

Of course, this doesn't mean we should stop acquiring new customers, because without new customers we wouldn't have a business. The point I'm making is this: The hidden profit center in your business is to sell more products, more often, and at higher prices to your *existing* customers.

If acquiring new customers is the "front end" of your business, selling to existing customers is the "back end" of your business. The natural tendency of most entrepreneurs is to focus extensively on acquiring new customers, rather than selling more to existing customers.

If this sounds like you, you're giving up a huge financial opportunity by not focusing more on existing customers. I'll explain why in a moment, but the short answer is this: 80 percent of your expenses come from activities related to acquiring and serving new customers, yet 80 percent of your profits come from selling more to existing customers.

In today's very crowded marketplace, it is difficult and expensive to stand out among your competitors. The unique, compelling, credible promise really helps you cut through the clutter, but even then people don't find out about your promise accidentally. It takes a deliberate effort and cost to get your promise in front of the right kind of prospect. This process consumes financial resources.

When you make that initial sale to a new customer, the revenue you generate from that sale has to cover many of your expenses. That one sale has to cover the costs of the product or service delivered. It has to pay for the marketing that was responsible for acquiring that customer. It also has to pay for your overhead (rent, utilities, etc.).

That's a lot of expenses that need to be covered by that initial sale.

In contrast, when you sell to existing customers, there is no customer acquisition cost. Usually, you don't have to expand your overhead by much (no new buildings, no new office equipment).

As a result, the expenses that need to be covered by the second, third, or fourth sale to an existing customer are much lower.

For example, suppose you sell your customer a $100 widget. Here's how the math might typically work out on the initial sale:

Initial Sale with Customer

$100 price
- $50 cost of widget
- $20 advertising
- $20 salaries, rent, utilities, taxes

$10 net profit

Let's assume you take the same customer you just sold the $100 widget to and turn around the next day and sell that same customer another $100 widget.

Keep in mind you have already acquired the customer, so your advertising cost is minimal. In addition, since your first sale covered the cost of your overhead, you don't really need to grow your infrastructure to sell more to this customer again.

Here's what that looks like:

Second Sale with Same Customer

$100 price
- $50 cost of widget
- $2 advertising
- $0 salaries, rent, utilities, taxes

$48 net profit

This second sale is 4.8 times more profitable than the
initial sale. This is an enormous profit opportunity that
most entrepreneurs miss entirely. For most businesses you
can easily double or triple the profit of the business just
by working on this one opportunity. Keep in mind, I did
not say double or triple the revenue of the business, but
rather the take-home profit you can spend. That's because
sales to existing customers are so much more profitable
than the initial sale that you don't need all that many
follow-up sales to dramatically increase your take-home
pay.

Here's a comparison of two scenarios. In example A,
your company focuses 100 percent on selling to new
customers. It gets a new customer, makes one sale to him,
then doesn't bother doing anything else with the
customer.

In example B, your company has figured out the
enormous profit potential of selling more to existing
customers, so it deliberately works on making sure every
customer it acquires is offered a chance to buy additional
products and services. Even though it tries to get every
first-time customer to be a repeat customer, it is only

successful one out of five attempts (or 20 percent of the time). Let's take a look at the impact this has on bottom-line take-home profits.

Example A – 5 new customers, 5 initial sales

Revenue	Profit
$100 initial sale	$10
$100 initial sale	$10
$100 initial sale	$10
$100 initial sale	$10
$100 initial sale	$10
$500 Revenue	**$50 Profit**

Example B – 5 new customers, 5 initial sales + 1 second sale

Revenue	Profit
$100 initial sale	$10
$100 initial sale	$10
$100 initial sale	$10
$100 initial sale	$10
$100 initial sale	$10
$100 second sale	**$48**
$600 Revenue	**$98 Profit**

Just by getting one out of every five new customers to place another order, you nearly double the profit of the business. That's a dramatic improvement to your income for what seems like a very simple change.

Let's go one step further. Instead of only successfully getting one out of every five new customers to buy again, let's say you're able to get two out of every five customers to make a second purchase.

Example C – 5 new customers, 5 initial sales + 2 second sales

Revenue	Profit
$100 initial sale	$10
$100 initial sale	$10
$100 initial sale	$10
$100 initial sale	$10
$100 initial sale	$10
$100 second sale	**$48**
$100 second sale	**$48**
$700 Revenue	**$146 Profit**

Now you've nearly tripled the income from your business. But wait, it gets even better. Who said you have to stop at getting just the second sale? What if for every two second sales you make, you get a third sale too? Here's what that would look like:

Example D – 5 new customers, 5 initial sales + 2 second sales + 1 third sale

Revenue	Profit
$100 initial sale	$10
$100 initial sale	$10
$100 initial sale	$10
$100 initial sale	$10
$100 initial sale	$10
$100 second sale	**$48**
$100 second sale	**$48**
$100 third sale	**$48**
$800 Revenue	**$194 Profit**

Compare Example A with Example D. The difference in these examples shows a fourfold improvement in your business income. That's a really big number that's very hard to ignore. Let's talk about four different ways you can sell more to existing customers.

Four Ways to Sell More to Existing Customers

Strategy #1:
The Up-sell

The first way to sell more to an existing customer is to offer the customer an up-sell of a larger quantity of what he just purchased immediately after he agrees to the initial order. The simplest example of an up-sell is one that I hear at McDonald's. After you order a soft drink or a side order of French fries, the cashier immediately asks you, "Would you like to supersize that for only 45 cents more?"

When I go to the movies and order a small popcorn, the person taking my order always asks, "Would you like to upgrade to a medium popcorn for only 25 cents more? It's twice as much popcorn for only 25 cents." Considering my small popcorn costs $4, getting twice as much for a quarter seems like such an irresistible deal, I say yes.

On a side note, for a long time I wondered why I would go to the movies intending to spend $8 but walk out having spent $20. I started studying popcorn and soft drink prices at the theaters and noticed that over the years, the theaters have deliberately engineered their prices to make the up-sell more attractive. They raise the price of the small popcorn to make the price difference between small and medium look very attractive, and they sell a lot more medium popcorns than they used to sell.

The easiest way to implement an up-sell is when you take a customer's order, whether it's at a cash register, over the phone, or across the desk, give your customer the option to buy a larger quantity of what he or she just ordered. Make it an irresistible deal.

- An up-sell can work in almost any business.

- If you sell tax preparation services, sell the customer next year's tax return service on the spot for a discount.

- If you run a restaurant and someone orders a steak, offer him or her a larger steak for just a few dollars more.

- If you're a retailer, offer the customer a "buy two get one free" deal, or a "buy five get one free" deal.

- If you provide consulting services, offer to extend your contract for an extra month and provide a financial incentive to do so.

In my own use of up-selling, I find that between 10 and 35 percent of customers will take the up-sell and pay for the higher-priced option of what you're offering. Keep in mind: The extra money from the up-sell is almost free money. All it takes is quite literally an extra 30 seconds of your order taker's time to offer the up-sell, and you'll get a few customers who say yes.

One more thing I've also found from my own extensive use and tracking of up-selling is that customers who take the up-sell tend to refund less often than those who don't, and they also end up spending more money with you over the next few months. I'm not 100 percent sure why this is the case, but my own tracking of my sales has proven this to be true for my business. In addition, my comparison of sales measures with other businesses I'm familiar with, that also track their sales, shows the same thing. My best guess is that by taking the up-sell option, it deepens customers' psychological commitment to your business and makes them better customers. After all, the only logical reason they would take the up-sell from you is if they mentally decided yours was a company worth doing business with.

Strategy #2:
The Cross-Sell

The next strategy to sell more to existing customers also happens within seconds of their agreement to make their initial purchase from you. In this strategy, rather than offering customers more of what they just purchased (as in an up-sell), you offer them a related product instead.

The classic example once again comes from McDonald's. When you order a hamburger, the cashier asks, "Would you like fries with that?" That's a cross- sell.

There is a lesson here. McDonald's became a Fortune 500 company for a reason. One of the reasons is it has mastered the art and science of up-selling and cross-selling.

Another example of cross-selling occurs when you go to a car dealer to buy a new car. These days, consumers are so savvy with figuring out dealer costs that they negotiate hard on the selling price of the car. You haggle with the sales rep. He calls in his manager, and you haggle some more, threaten to walk out, talk to the manager some more, and after three hours of tough negotiations you settle on a price. The sales rep then shakes your hand, tells you that you worked him over good, that he's barely making a profit on this thing, and to go talk to Joan in the back office to take care of the paperwork.

You're patting yourself on the back, excited that you got a great deal, and as Joan hands you the paperwork, she asks, "Would you like the leather seating option?" And you say, "Oh, yeah. Sure, why not?" Then she asks, "Would you like our no hassle, no maintenance package? We'll pay for all your oil changes and wash your car for two years," and you say, "Oh, yeah, that sounds great. I'll take it." Then Joan asks, "Would you like to add an extended warranty for a total of seven years of no repair bills?" Of course, you say, "That would be great." Then Joan asks about financing packages and offers you insurance for your car.

It only occurs to you after the fact that Joan cross-sold you left and right and made a profit of thousands in the process. Actually, many years ago I had a client who was a major lender in the automobile financing industry. And if I recall correctly, at the time, auto dealers made very little profit on the sale of new cars. They made one-third of their profit from "finance and insurance" (e.g., from Joan), another third of their profit from "service and repairs," and the final one-third from "selling used cars." The core business of selling new cars was simply a break-even business that fed customers into the cross-selling of finance, insurance, and repair.

For auto dealers, *none* of the profit comes from the actual selling of new cars. All the profit from new car sales comes from the cross-selling of related offers, but not from the car itself.

Once again, the easiest way to implement a cross-sell is to make customers an offer for a related product immediately after they agree to the initial order. This can happen over the phone, in person, at the cash register, or across the table as the customer is signing a contract. Whereas the up-sell only works in some businesses, the cross-sell definitely works in every business.

Here are a few examples:

- If you sell a tax return service, sell a tax reduction planning program to help customers prepare their taxes for next year.

- If you install air conditioning systems (or any kind of equipment), offer an extended warranty or a "we'll do it for you" maintenance program (just like the auto dealers).

- If you run a restaurant and someone orders an entrée, cross-sell wine, appetizers, side orders, dessert, and coffee.

- If you sell a professional service or consulting services, when your client agrees to hire you to solve problem X, ask him if he needs help with problem Y or Z too.

- If you're a retailer, offer the client something that is used with the product he just purchased. If it's an electronic device, cross-sell batteries, a carrying case, A/C adapter, or car power adapter. If it's a shirt, cross-sell the pants, a tie (if it's for a guy), or a necklace or earrings (if it's for a woman).

- If you're a dentist fixing someone's cavity, have your receptionist cross-sell the next checkup and get the client to pay for it in advance (reminding him that if he hadn't skipped his checkup, he wouldn't have had the cavity).

- If you run a bagel shop, cross-sell a cup of coffee.

- If you're a travel agent, cross-sell trip insurance along with any tickets you book for your clients.

- If you're an insurance agent, cross-sell auto insurance and life insurance.

- If you sell lawn care services, cross-sell an option to re-landscape certain parts of your customers' lawns.

- If you sell plumbing repair services, sell a plumbing problem prevention service, audit, or evaluation.

The possibilities are endless. If you're still scratching your head wondering what you can cross- sell, here are a few tips:

- Think about what activities your customers engage in immediately *before* using your product/service. What products or service do they use to perform this activity?

- What else do they need when they use your product or service to make their experience easier, faster, or better? Could you provide that product or service too?

- Think about what activities your customers engage in immediately *after* using your product/service. What products or service do they use to perform this activity?

If you only sell one product or service, consider partnering with providers of a related product or service and cross-sell their offer for them in exchange for a financial incentive. Or you can flip it around and have the partners cross-sell your products or service to their customers.

There is a lot of money to be made in cross-selling, and I strongly encourage you to think about the infinite cross-selling opportunities that are readily available to you in your business.

Strategy #3:
The Immediate Follow-on Sale

Another strategy for getting more sales from existing customers is to make your first-time buyers an offer a few days after they make their initial order. If you've ever bought anything via mail order or on the Internet and the company shipped you a box, you'll notice that oftentimes inside the box is not just your product but also a flyer or even a catalog of other things you can buy from them.

That's an immediate follow-on sale.

Generally speaking, after customers make their initial purchase from you, there's a window of opportunity where they really like what you have to offer. Take advantage of that opportunity and make it easy for them to buy more stuff from you.

Pretty much anything you can cross-sell at the moment you take the customer's order, you can also offer as an immediate follow-on sale a few days later.

If you're the auto dealer and the customer didn't take the hassle-free maintenance package from Joan, you can have Joan call a week later, thank the customer for his business, and offer the hassle-free maintenance package again.

This same immediate follow-on sale can be used by a dentist to presell the next checkup, the tax preparer to sell a proactive tax planning service, the restaurant to presell a special event it's having next month, the insurance agent to sell a life insurance policy a few days after selling an auto insurance policy.

This works for several reasons.

If your products and services are really good, the new customers will only figure this out for themselves *after* they make the initial purchase. Whereas they weren't 100 percent certain about the quality of your product or service when they bought it, after using it for a few days they really love you and your company. Because of this, sometimes customers are more likely to buy a few days after the sale rather than taking an up-sell or cross-sell right at the point of the initial sale.

Another reason is sometimes it doesn't occur to them initially that they need this additional product or service.

Maybe you offer a cross-sell when they make their initial order, but they don't take it. But a few days later, they say to themselves, "Hmm ... actually, that wasn't a bad idea. I see how that could help now." Only a few people would go out of their way to contact you to get whatever it is you offered them. However, if you made it really easy for them to get a "second chance" offer, a lot of them will take it.

There is a lot of opportunity to make a lot more money with the immediate follow-on sale. The latest opportunity I've spotted has to do with children's shoes. We have a young daughter who's growing really fast. One of the consequences of this is that she's constantly outgrowing her shoes. We visit the shoe store every few months.

It's a big pain for several reasons. Most of the shoes aren't comfortable – they're too stiff, too tall, and too bulky or have some extra flap in the wrong place that makes them uncomfortable to wear. So we have to get my daughter to try on many different pairs. A few months later, we have to repeat the process. But to make things worse, a year later when we need a similar type of shoe for that season (like winter shoes), all the models that were around last year have been discontinued. So we have to repeat the whole process again.

My wife started doing something that I thought was very clever. Once we find a shoe that my daughter likes, she buys the exact same shoe one, two, and sometimes three sizes larger. That way we've got the shoe thing covered for the next two to three years. Sure, there is some risk to this approach, but we just hate shoe shopping so much that it's worth it.

That got me thinking that, knowing my wife, she came up with this idea all by herself. But why didn't the shoe store itself offer us this idea? We don't buy shoes for our daughter; we're buying "protected, comfortable feet" for her. Had our shoe store called us a week later, asked us how the shoes were doing on my daughter and whether we wanted the store to ship us the next three sizes to save us the hassle of coming back over and over again, there's a very good chance we would have said yes. Instead, my wife just found the same shoes in the larger sizes and ordered them on the Internet to avoid having to make the long drive to the shoe store, which, as you guessed, she and I both hate doing.

That's the immediate follow-on sale. It's a "hidden" profit opportunity that most businesses never use because it's not always obvious. However, now that you're aware of it, I would encourage you to find ways to offer an immediate follow-on sale to your customers.

Strategy #4:
The Continuity Sale

The final strategy for making more money from existing customers is my hands-down favorite. This one strategy has been responsible for more of my net profits than any other and requires very little work once you get it set up. It's called the "continuity sale."

The continuity sale is simply to provide some product or service on an ongoing basis via a monthly subscription.

The product or service is provided continuously to your customers until they cancel it. The advantage of continuity sales is, with continuous delivery of products and services to your customers, you gain the enormous financial advantage of automatic, recurring, continuous billing of your customers.

Your cable, telephone, and electricity bills are all continuously delivered services with continuous billing. If you're familiar with the fruit of the month club, then you've seen a continuity sale. If you've seen the 12 CDs for just one penny music club offer that sends you a new CD each month, then you're familiar with another continuity program. The same goes for the book of the month club. The great thing about these programs from the business's point of view: Once you get customers in there, they are in there forever or until they cancel.

More recent innovations include NetFlix and Blockbuster introducing their video rental membership program. Rather than renting a video one at a time, you are charged a monthly fee, and you can borrow as many as you want for a fixed, monthly, recurring charge.

Earlier in this chapter, I walked you through examples of the extraordinary profit increases that can come from selling to existing customers. You'll recall that the second and third sales are often five times more profitable than the first sale – particularly when you consider all the advertising and overhead the first sale must support.

The reason I recommend finding ways to incorporate continuity or recurring revenue programs into your business is that it stabilizes operating cash flow. It makes a portion of your revenue very predictable – a nice thing to have in a recession.

In addition to stability, continuity programs can provide incredible profits to your business. This is because properly marketed and designed continuity programs get more return out of your initial investment to acquire a new customer.

Most business owners don't focus nearly as hard on getting the second sale (the most profitable sale) as they do on the first sale (the least profitable sale). As I mentioned earlier, getting second, third, and fourth sales from a customer you've already acquired with your investment of time and money is critical to generating the maximum cash flow from your business. This is especially crucial in a recession. You can't afford to not get the largest possible return on any investment you make in your business.

When your business offers a continuity program of some type and you have a deliberate approach to get your first-time customers into it, you set yourself up for significantly higher profits, greater income stability, and less work.

If there were ever an example of working smarter and not harder, continuity programs would be it. Here's the key insight to keep in mind. The most difficult, most time consuming, most expensive activity in your business is acquiring customers. The least difficult, least time consuming, least expensive activity in your business is selling more stuff to customers you've already acquired. It's simply an inefficient use of your time and money to focus exclusively on new customer acquisition at the expense of serving existing customers. The whole purpose of going to the effort to acquire customers is so you can do the easy part of selling more to them.

Here's another way to think of it. When I was growing up, my mom would not let me eat dessert until I ate my vegetables. To this day, I still prefer eating ice cream to asparagus. When you structure your entire business to focus on customer acquisition, it's like eating asparagus for every meal and deliberately declining the ice cream treat afterward. The whole point of eating the asparagus is so you can eat the ice cream. You tolerate the asparagus to get to the ice cream. It makes absolutely no sense to tolerate the asparagus and **not** eat the ice cream. As my daughter would say, "That's silly."

So don't be silly! You need to find a way to sell more to existing customers, and implementing continuity programs is hands down the single most profitable, easiest way to do that.

Getting Started with Continuity Programs

Let's say you're interested in continuity programs and the recurring revenue stream they provide, but you can't possibly see how your business lends itself to a continuity program.

Let me show you several examples of ordinary businesses that can be converted into continuity income businesses. For each example, I will show a specific business and one option to generate a continuity income stream from it. Then I'll extract the general lesson from the example that you can apply to your business.

Example #1 – Same Service, Same Price, Predictable Purchase Schedule

I get my oil changed at a local oil change shop. I try to get in there every 3,000 miles like they suggest but I often don't get in until 6,000 miles. Sometimes I might be on the road when it occurs to me to change the oil and instead of going to my local oil change place, I might just use a competitor if that happens to be near when I remember I need the oil changed.

To this company's credit, it puts a little sticker on my windshield to remind me of when I need to come back and usually sends me a postcard with a coupon every 90 days. But, if the shop looked at my service record, it would know that between the two cars we own, I've done business with it 16 times in the past four years. If it also looked more carefully, it would have noticed that had I done business with it exclusively at the recommended times, I should have done business with the shop 32 times!

Instead of trying to resell me on using its oil change service every 90 days, it should just enroll me on an "oil change subscription program" or "oil change hassle free maintenance program." Instead of trying to get $60 out of me every 90 days (which it is rarely successful in doing), it should offer me a discount to become a member where I pay $17 per month per car for up to four oil changes per year included for free.

This kind of program "locks" me into doing business with it. Once I'm a member, it would be foolish for me to go get an oil change somewhere else when the oil change is "free" at my favorite oil change place. Using this approach even with the discount, it would generate $204 per year from me for four oil changes whereas now it only gets two oil changes a year from me for $120. That's a 70 percent increase in revenue right off the bat. In addition, "members" tend to be better customers and buy other products and services too. Once it has got me coming in regularly, it can up-sell me on upgrading wiper blades, maintaining the radiator, and whatever other stuff they do to make my car run trouble free.

This is essentially a maintenance contract that is very common among large companies that have expensive equipment that needs to be maintained. If your business provides some type of service that is performed regularly for your customers, you could very easily use this model. Here are several businesses that could use this model:

- Barber
- Hair salon
- Beauty salon (manicure, pedicure)
- Heating and ventilation contractor (duct cleaning)
- Maid service
- Carpet cleaning
- Window cleaning
- Car wash

- Dentist (2 times per year teeth cleaning plus annual checkup)
- Health club
- Yoga studio
- Tax preparation services

When I mention this list to many entrepreneurs, they are initially surprised because they didn't think of these businesses as lending themselves to being a continuity income business.

What most of these businesses have in common is that most of the clients have a preferred vendor, someone they usually do business with out of habit, loyalty, or laziness. What these businesses also have in common is most of their customers don't do business with them as often as they could or should. For example, I try to get a haircut every three weeks, but I don't. I try to get my car washed every month, but I don't. I try to work out every day, but I don't. In all of these situations, I actually prefer to spend money with these businesses, but for a number of reasons I don't.

The more forgetful I become, the busier I become; and the more lazy I become as a customer, the **less** money each of these businesses makes from me. Now let's flip it around. If all these businesses had membership programs and provided an incentive to join them (either a one-time gift just to try it, or some type of ongoing financial incentive), there's a good chance I would join several such programs.

Once I become a member, the more forgetful I am, the busier I am, the lazier I become, instead of the business making *less* money, the business actually now makes *more* money. That's because they make their money off of my monthly membership fee instead of when I visit their place of business or engage them in doing business with me somehow. It's like the local health club – their most profitable customers (usually me!) are the ones who pay every month but do NOT go in to work out.

Example #2 – Different Products/Service, Different Prices, Frequent but Irregular Purchase Schedule

Continuity income streams can also be developed for businesses where what customers buy, how much they spend, and when they do business with you varies a lot. A fairly typical example would be that of a restaurant. Every meal is different (sometimes it's two people, other times it's three or four people); what the customer orders is different; the check amount is different; and customers usually don't come in on a set schedule. A situation like this can still lend itself to adopting a continuity income stream.

You could create a frequent diners program or a VIP diners program. Your clients pay you a $100 per month membership fee, and in exchange they get $110 in gift certificates each month, preferred seating/reservations and one dessert or appetizer per meal is always free. They are getting a great deal and 80 percent of the time they're going to spend *more* than the $110 in gift certificates each month anyway. For the restaurant, if they could sign up just 70 customers into this program, that's $7,000 in credit card revenue they generate on the first of the month – that's a pretty good way to start off the month!

For a customer who likes the restaurant, it's a great deal all the way around. It also provides a big incentive to keep going back to the same restaurant whenever you're going out. Frankly, I hate the conversation I have with my wife every weekend that goes like this, "Where do you want to go out to eat?" "I don't know … where do you want to go out to eat?" Invariably, it's a 10-minute discussion, but if we were members somewhere and had a "default" choice, we'd probably just go there.

You could use a similar approach for any retail store – clothing, toys, groceries, auto parts – you simply provide a monthly membership program where the customer's first $X of spending is free (and usually equal to their monthly membership fees) then provide them with some additional one-time or ongoing incentive where it makes more sense to join the program than not join it.

Examples of businesses that can use this approach:

- Any retail store that sells consumables or frequently used items (pet store, groceries, auto parts, crafts)

- Any restaurant

- Any mail order business that sells consumables or frequently used items

Example #3 – Product or Service Business with Infrequent Purchase Schedule

Continuity programs can also be created for service businesses where your clients use your service infrequently. Examples that come to mind are real estate agents, mortgage brokers, consulting firms, attorneys, and auto dealers. The customers don't require your product or service very often—typically, it's for a high-ticket transaction. In these situations, the business makes so much money from the one-time, infrequent transaction, that it usually generates more income than a continuity program.

In these cases, the value of the continuity program has less to do with the income from the continuity program itself and more with making sure you get the next big transaction from those customers when their next big purchasing need comes along. The key to becoming the default provider, or the person the customers refer their friends to, is to stay in front of the customers constantly.

An easy way to do this is to start a monthly newsletter that covers topics that are of interest to your best customers. For example, if you're a real estate agent, you could publish a monthly newsletter about your favorite restaurants in the area, review local businesses (e.g., best hair salon, best car wash), tips on how to increase the value of the person's home, how to sell or buy the customer's next home (with you, of course!), and how to refer clients to you.

The great thing about a monthly newsletter program that provides some personality and professional advice is it accomplishes two things. First, it helps the customer get to know you better – and people like to do business with people they know. Second, you continually establish and reinforce your position as an expert. Every month customers get to see firsthand how good you are at what you do.

You could offer this newsletter for just a few dollars every quarter or every year, and set it up so the subscription auto-renews on an ongoing basis until canceled. If the average ticket size for your service is really profitable, you might even want to provide this newsletter to your previous customers and hottest prospects for free. In this case, you're giving up the continuity income, but you've got a fantastic marketing program.

Part III:
Business Reinvention

CHAPTER 12

Business Reinvention

In a recession, especially a severe one, you face one of two decisions. Do you stay the course "as is" or do you make a big change? If you're in a smaller business, this decision applies to your whole business. In a larger company, this decision sometimes applies to a particular division or segment of your business.

If a recession has had minimal financial impact on your business, then staying the course in a more or less "as is" fashion with perhaps a few incremental improvements may be enough.

If your business, or segments of your business, has been hit hard, it's probably time to seriously consider making dramatic changes. Extreme times sometimes call for extreme measures.

In an extremely severe recession or depression, many times the risk of doing nothing is much higher than the risk of executing a well-thought-out change. It is probably one of the few times in an economic cycle where this is true. If a business is on track to pretty much fail, what's the worst thing that can happen if you try something different? Worst-case scenario: You still fail. Best-case scenario: You turn the whole thing around, survive, and, if you move fast enough, thrive.

Reinventing Your Business

When I've given speeches related to this book, the big takeaway that audiences walk away with is the need to reinvent one's business if its current form isn't working in a downturn.

When the economy evolves at a pace of 5 mph, having your business change at a pace of 10 mph is enough to keep pace with the times.

When an economy has gone through a massive structural shift, such as in a severe recession or any other major economic crisis, the pace of change in the economy suddenly speeds up to 50 mph.

Suddenly, the 10 mph pace of change that has served you well for years, or even decades, often becomes inadequate in an obvious way.

For some businesses that dodged the brunt of the economic shift, only a modest change is needed to survive in a recession.

For other businesses, the impact of the recession may be more significant, and a more dramatic solution is required. That solution is to reinvent parts of or all of your business.

So where does one start in the reinvention process?

It's Not Rocket Science:
Follow the Money

The reinvention process is conceptually very simple. Follow the money. Phrased differently, you want your products, services, and company to be in alignment with how buyers are spending their money right now – not last year, but right now.

In some markets, buyers have made massive changes in their spending priorities. If you're in such a market, there's a strong chance that your business is out of alignment with buyers' current spending patterns.

Until you've figured out where the money **is** being spent, it is pretty much pointless to do anything else. Developing products and services that don't match customer spending priorities is a waste of time and money. Trying to sell and market harder to an audience that fundamentally doesn't care about what you offer is equally pointless.

You absolutely, positively, must get a grasp of what your customers are thinking and where they *are* spending money. In some cases, you may be forced to find an entirely different set of customers who are interested in what you have to offer.

When I speak with a new client, I can usually tell if the business is going to make it in its "as is" form. If the business, product line, or division of the business is bleeding cash, it's obvious it's not working. Customers vote with their wallets and the results are crystal clear – just look at your bank account.

But the harder question to figure out is if what you're doing now isn't working, then what will work? This is of course the million-dollar question and is probably the point at which people who become my clients seek me out. They know enough to know their current path isn't working, and while they sense the business, product, or service has potential, somehow all the pieces aren't lining up in the right way to produce sales.

The Two Components for Business Reinvention

In these situations, the big question is to figure out whether or not the business can be turned around easily and quickly. There are two key factors that I use to make this determination.

1. **Potential for a New "Recipe":** Can the "raw ingredients" of the company (its target customer, product/service, sales/marketing model) be used in a new combination, or "recipe," to better match what buyers are spending on?

2. **Uniqueness:** Does the business have anything unique going for it?

Think of a company's unique assets or "raw ingredients" as its products, services, sales/distribution method, customer lists, and market intelligence. I look to see if the same ingredients can be rearranged into a different combination or "recipe" to fall in line with new market demand.

Focus on this area first because trying to create a new asset when time, money, and resources are limited is very difficult to do. Creating a new product to sell takes time. Trying to build a different sales model, say, moving from in-person sales to direct mail, takes time to establish.

This process of creating a new "recipe" that combines the company's existing assets in a new way is part art and part science. The science part comes from knowing the numbers in your business and spotting promising trends hiding just beneath the surface. Sometimes this trend might be noticing that one product is selling modestly well despite no marketing or sales effort. Other times, it's noticing that one type of customer is really easy to please, buys constantly, but for one reason or another isn't the type of customer the business is focusing on attracting.

The artistry comes from interpreting this factual data in the context of market demand, the company's strengths, and the CEO's comfort zone to find the right "recipe" to make the business work with the least risk, lowest investment, and greatest speed. It's part art and part science.

A part of this business reinvention process includes looking for something unique in the business that can be harnessed more effectively. I call this looking for the unpolished diamond in the business. This can be anything from the owner's Rolodex, a unique back story behind the business, a neglected customer list, a great product that's trapped behind the wrong distribution system, or any number of things.

To launch a business reinvention effectively, it often requires an injection of immediate cash flow into the business. Since many businesses in need of reinvention are typically cash flow challenged, the cash flow boost needs to come from operations. When the company has an underutilized asset, it takes only a modest bit of effort to exploit that ignored asset.

While a business that lacks uniqueness can still be turned around, the process is more difficult and the company may not be able to sustain the progress. Sooner or later uniqueness is going to be critical. So it's best to spot the uniqueness and build around it early in the reinvention process.

Once you have a new business reinvention recipe in mind, it's time to move to the next step in the process. Now you want to test your idea against the harsh reality of the real world marketplace. Great ideas are just that … ideas. As I mentioned previously, it doesn't matter if you think it's a great idea. It only matters if the people with the money – the buyers – think it's a good idea.

The process of testing interesting reinvention ideas against marketplace reality is even more challenging in a severe recession. Customers themselves may not have clarity around their own spending priorities. They may be waiting to see how their own customers' spending priorities have changed. In consumer markets, consumers are trying to get a gauge on their job security and net worth, both of which may be in flux.

For these reasons, it's vital to rely on a process to validate against marketplace reality. It's precisely in times where spending priorities, and thus the economy, are in flux that it is prudent to avoid using only gut instinct. While gut instinct can work, it is during times of transition when it is most likely to be wrong.

Supplier-Driven versus Customer-Driven Business Reinvention

The golden rule of business reinvention is this. It does not matter one bit what you want to sell. It only matters what customers want to buy!

Most companies use a supplier-driven process to figure out what products and services they offer to the marketplace. Far too many businesses are operated on the business principle that "I got a great idea and I want to sell X to customers."

This is a high-risk approach. It can be appropriate in certain industries, such as high-tech, where the innovation is so new and different that customers have a very hard time understanding whether or not they would want the product. But in most industries, deciding you want to sell X because you think it's a great idea is risky.

Personally, I don't like taking big risks when it's not necessary. Instead, going after a "sure thing" – or something as close to it as possible – makes more sense. Rather than taking a supplier-driven approach where the vendor decides what he or she wants to sell, I prefer a customer-demand driven process.

The idea is fairly simple. Figure out what customers are willing to buy and then give it to them. It sounds like common sense, but I cannot tell you how rare this kind of thinking is. I've had countless conversations with business owners and CEOs who are trying to force their idea of a good product or service onto customers who totally disagree. At the end of the day, the person who is voting with his or her wallet wins.

When the economy undergoes a massive structural shift, as it does in a recession, the odds that gut instinct and a supplier-driven approach are wrong are much higher. The rules of the game have changed, and it's pointless to try to win a game whose rules you don't understand. Better to figure out those rules by figuring out what customers want first.

But this is especially difficult to do in a recession. In an economy in flux, transition, or even chaos, it's very hard to figure out what's *really* going on.

The Fog of War
(And Recessions)

Military leaders use a phrase called the "fog of war" to describe what happens to their best laid battle plans once the fighting begins. Things happen so fast. The information coming back from the front lines is often incomplete and outdated. In the chaos of war, with thousands of people and weapons moving around in different directions, it's hard to figure out something as simple as who's your friend and who's your foe.

As evidence of this, one of the main reasons for "friendly fire" accidents where, say, a US marine accidentally shoots and kills a fellow marine is this fog of war effect.

Well, running a business in a recession comes with it its own fog. When customer demand is being reprioritized and recalibrated throughout the whole economy, it's very confusing and disorienting.

That's because our economy is very interconnected. Companies are waiting to see how consumer spending patterns shake out. Consumers are concerned about layoffs and are waiting to see how employers respond. Of course, companies are employers and consumers are employees. In this circular process, everyone in the economy is looking at everyone else in the economy before deciding what to do. This of course creates a weird analysis paralysis phenomenon.

This is the fog of a recession – trying to recalibrate your sales, marketing, and product development efforts to be in line with your customers' spending priorities when they are trying to do the same thing themselves.

This additional level of complexity during a recession is something you need to be aware of. To deal with this "fog" you need some mechanism or process to figure out what the heck is going on out there in the marketplace.

On the one hand, a supplier-driven process to business reinvention has a very low chance of success in a recession. On the other hand, a customer-driven reinvention process makes more sense but you have to deal with this "fog" problem. So what's the right answer?

The Winning Recalibration Process

To see through the fog that comes with a recession, you need a method to identify clearly what customers are doing and what they want. You need the equivalent of a pair of X-ray vision glasses so that you can see clearly through the fog.

The equivalent of X-ray vision glasses is a systematic process for recalibrating your decisions, plans, and assumptions with customers whose needs and behaviors are continually evolving.

The challenge with the demand-driven process is the fact that it's a process. You start with what you know, come up with your best concept for reinvention, but still need to find some way to cheaply validate it with real customers before investing a lot into it.

Invariably, you never get it right the first time. You get some feedback from the customers: Perhaps they like one particular aspect of your reinvented business, product, or service, but they absolutely and positively hate another aspect. Okay, let's listen to them. And then make another attempt.

It is through this iterative process of market testing that one can rack up a very high success rate. I call this the "Victor Process" – it is both a play on my first name and also refers to the idea that it's the process that winning businesses adopt to continuously increase sales and profits in any economy.

This process allows you to calibrate how closely your business is aligned to market demand (Rule #2) and how unique what you have to offer is in the eyes of your buyers (Rule #3). Remember, it's not good enough to be in alignment with market demand if you don't have something unique to offer. Similarly, it's not good enough to offer a unique solution to a problem buyers don't care about. You have to do *both*. You must align to market demand *and* do so in a unique way at the same time.

This is impossible to get right on the first attempt. I've been using this process in my own business and that of clients for years. And it is never, ever right the first time. That's why it's a process.

But the purpose of the process is to recalibrate your efforts to see how closely they align with what buyers are willing to spend money on. And then to determine whether or not *they*, not you, see anything unique about what you're offering.

Remember, your opinion, while interesting, is not relevant. It's only the opinions and spending behaviors of customers that matter. When customers vote with their wallet, they vote honestly. Any other time, things like being polite, telling you what you want to hear, or avoiding hurting your feelings comes into play. But the second that real money, their money, is at stake, the truth comes out.

When I coach clients, I try to impress this concept upon them. For any decision that requires customer buy-in to succeed, I never tell clients that a specific strategy will work. That's because, in most cases, I'm not their target customer – and I have to remind them that they aren't either.

Instead, I do say that the last three clients who used a particular strategy saw a financial improvement between 15 and 35 percent. Or I'll say when I used this strategy in my own business in this situation, it produced a 25 percent improvement. While all this suggests there's a very likely chance it'll work for a client, you never **really** know until you try it. And that's why it's a process. Until the customer votes with his wallet, everything else is really just educated guessing.

Many companies are unaccustomed to operating in this way. So getting your company to adopt this approach requires not only a process change, but a mind-set and culture change as well. In coaching clients on implementing this approach, I've found the mind-set shift and culture change to be the most critical to long-term success, but it also requires the most effort to change.

For more tips on this winning process, visit www.victorprocess.com.

Why the World's Greatest Heart Surgeons Don't Operate on Themselves

The world's greatest heart surgeons don't operate on themselves because they are too close to the problem to solve it!

The heart surgeon's dilemma occurs because of both a physical limitation as well as limitation of perspective. It's this latter thing, perspective, that's relevant to your business.

Most business owners and CEOs are "too close" to their own business to see it objectively. They're too familiar with their own business. They know the industry too well. And their memory of why the current approach used to work a few years ago is too good. They're too used to the assumptions they made about their businesses

– assumptions that were unconsciously made and solidified in their minds in the midst of a booming economy that no longer exists.

Being "too close" causes all kinds of problems. If you have a great, but under-utilized asset, you may be too used to ignoring it – because it's how you've always done things. Or a small problem can creep up on you over a long period of time. Being close to the business, you never noticed the tiny changes occurring from week to week and thus missed the cumulative magnitude of the problem that has emerged over time. Someone with a fresh set of eyes and an unbiased perspective can spot this kind of problem in a few minutes whereas you're too used to it to notice it.

It's kind of like raising young children. Day to day they don't change that much. But month to month they do. So if you have friends or family who see your young kids every few months, they're going to remark at how much they've changed since the last visit – when you barely noticed a thing.

Someone who's competent, is emotionally uninvolved in your business, and doesn't have psychological ties or a memory of your company's past can challenge assumptions you're making about your business – assumptions that may no longer be true in the current economic environment.

If you sense that some degree of business reinvention is needed in your business, it's very useful to include a competent outside advisor in the process. You want to ensure that this outsider is someone with a history of dealing with the kinds of issues you are facing and has experience overcoming those issues.

When the Rules of the Game Change The Person Who Doesn't Remember the Old Rules Is an Asset

I find that the outsider role is especially critical in the time of a major transition. When a business is running well without any major problems, the problems that do emerge usually come with simple and obvious solutions. Similarly, under normal "status quo" circumstances where the business isn't under any major outside pressure, the opportunities that present themselves are also fairly obvious.

The real challenge comes in times of crisis or extreme changes in market forces. When the rules of the game change, it is **very** disorienting. The process of recalibrating to market demand is confusing. This is one time when deep experience in your business and industry can be a liability.

When you're good at operating your business under the rules of the prerecession economy, it can be difficult to make the transition to the new rules of game. In this case, having someone you can rely on who is not emotionally involved in your business, has no memory of your company's glorious past (in a boom economy), and looks only at the cold hard facts of the current situation is a good idea.

This person has no ties to the business's past and has no emotional attachment to the future dreams for the business that may have been shattered or delayed. This person is forced to just look at the present. What is true (or not true) about this business right now? This is the foundation you must have to make well-informed decisions about your business.

If you don't understand the problems in your business correctly, it's possible for any solution to succeed. Sure, you may succeed in solving the wrong problem – but that hardly helps your business.

Having an outsider with fresh eyes, relevant experience, and judgment you trust involved in the decision-making cycle is a vital part of the business reinvention process. This person can ideally provide a clinical, totally objective, and emotionally uninvolved perspective that's especially helpful in a chaotic and disorienting economy.

Business Reinvention Tips and Resources

In the next chapter, I'll share some tips and resources that you may find helpful in jump-starting the business reinvention process.

CHAPTER 13

Resources for Business Reinvention

Reinventing a business forces you to think and act differently than you did before. The transition can be difficult to make. For most people, business reinvention is a one-time, or at least once-in-a-long-time, type of activity.

It's in these situations that seeking outside guidance from someone who constantly reinvents businesses on a weekly basis can be helpful. Here are some resources of mine that you may find useful. I'll share each one and explain what it is, and if one resonates with you, I suggest that you consider taking advantage of it.

Resource #1
Free Email Recession Survival Tips and Strategies

The first resource you should definitely take advantage of is my free email newsletter. My email articles and alerts provide tips, reminders, and case study examples of how to survive, and even thrive, in a recession.

I publish issues when I have something useful to say; otherwise I prefer to not waste your time. I hate it when people waste my time and especially hate it when useless email newsletters clutter my email inbox, don't add any value, and distract me from real work. This is a pet peeve of mine. So I aim to keep the issues in my newsletter actually useful – a refreshing change for you.

The other nice benefit of my free email newsletter is that I answer questions from readers. If you have a question, ask me. If you don't know what to do next in your business, ask me. Like a newspaper columnist, I write and publish my answers for all my readers to see. If your situation and question are specific to your business, I tend to restate the question so that the answer is useful not only to you, but to others as well.

To subscribe to this free newsletter, just visit www.askvictor.com. Notice that the website address reflects the spirit of the newsletter. When you don't know what to do, just "ask Victor."

If this sounds valuable to you, I would suggest visiting www.askvictor.com now while you still remember to do so.

Resource #2
Current Business Reinvention Case Studies

In this book, all the examples I provide are based on historical success stories. The natural tendency for some people is to assume that what has worked for the past 136 years might not work today.

To prove that it does work, I've assembled a number of case study videos of companies that have successfully reinvented themselves recently. These are small and medium-sized businesses that made dramatic improvements in their business during the recession that began in 2008.

These modern-day case studies have two commonalities. First, these business owners followed the four recession-proof rules covered in the first part of this book. The second commonality is that they are all very different from one another.

No two success stories are the same. They come from wildly different industries. Some are bigger companies. Others are smaller ones. But all of them are unique in their own ways. This is precisely the point I want to emphasize. The proven path to recession survival is to not take the most common path.

The video case studies I've assembled convey this key idea. To see how business owners like you successfully reinvented their businesses, visit www.victorprocess.com.

Resource #3:
Seminars, Tool Kits, and Home-Study Programs

If you are interested in acquiring more skills to recession-proof your business, you can find my resource library and a schedule of upcoming seminars at www.victorcheng.com. The resource library and event schedule are continually evolving to meet the needs of my clients and are kept up-to-date based on current economic conditions.

Feel free to visit www.victorcheng.com to see the current set of available resources. However, expect those resources to change.

To be alerted of changes without having to visit the website regularly, sign up for my email newsletter at www.askvictor.com, as major updates to my main website are announced in my newsletter from time to time.

Resource #4:
Individualized Business Coaching

Finally, I do provide business coaching services to business owners and CEOs who are fairly determined to ensure that their businesses survive a recession.

There is a wide range of coaching programs available. To request more information about these options, visit www.victorcheng.com/coaching.

Closing Thoughts

When I've given speeches about the topics discussed within this book, people often come up to me afterward to share what they thought were the big ideas from my talk. Invariably, the feedback tends to center around three key takeaways. Since it's a fitting way to recap everything we've covered, I thought I'd share them with you.

The first takeaway is that there really is hope for businesses to survive even the severest of recessions. This isn't cheerleading, rah rah, be enthusiastic for no good reason. The feeling of hope comes from the reassuring certainty provided by history, facts, and guidance.

The second takeaway is that you can't just sit back and take a recession passively. You have to be proactive, deliberately seek out opportunities, and adapt to new circumstances.

I've had people come up to me after a speech and tell me that in the middle of my talk they made major decisions about their businesses. Some decide to drop certain parts of their businesses, where the demand isn't there and they reluctantly admit they have nothing unique to offer, in order to focus on fledgling but much more promising opportunities where they see demand and a chance at offering something unique.

Other business owners tell me that their businesses have been doing well, but they aren't sure why they are doing well. Now that they understand the principles behind a recession-proof business and realize they have one, they've decided they're going to stop worrying for no good reason. Instead, they've decided on the spot to aggressively push their advantageous position rather than hunker down, which is what they thought they were "supposed" to do in a recession.

All this feedback encourages me. Because the overall lesson to this point is that taking proactive measures is much more likely to solve your problems than will passive worrying.

Finally, the last big takeaway is having the "aha" moment that reinventing your business is the solution to a business that's struggling because of a recession. The process of figuring out what your market wants right now (not two years ago), taking that information to heart, and reinventing your business around that new information seems to resonate with many people.

It helps them understand why their businesses, or parts of their businesses, are struggling. It also allows them to channel any anxious energy they have in a productive direction. If your business is outdated given the times, it's time to reinvent a "new" one to better match what buyers now want.

In closing, let me make a final comment. When I began writing this book, it was my goal to share stories and concepts that would open your eyes to an alternative perspective on running a business in a recession, provide you with some reassurance based on history, and be genuinely useful.

More than influencing how you think and feel about your business, it was my real hope to influence the actions you take in running your business – helping you survive if you're struggling, and encouraging you to be more aggressive if you're already doing well.

The downside of authorship is that it's historically a one-way communication medium. Did anyone read the book? Did anyone use it? Do they love it or hate it? And why? These are the questions we authors ask ourselves, but we rarely get complete answers. So I have a favor to ask of you. Email me at victor@victorcheng.com and send me your feedback (I'll take the good and the bad) and especially your success stories. And if you'd like to stay in touch, consider subscribing to my free email newsletter at www.askvictor.com.

Finally, I want to wish you the best of luck in creating your own recession-proof business.